ENDORSEMENTS

Further Along is Endorsed by the following respected leaders:

"Dan Brooks tells a story of grit, gratitude, faith, and resilience in the face of enormous health challenges. He unflinchingly details the daily tasks of carrying on in spite of a degenerative neuromuscular disease called multiple systems atrophy. For anyone facing this or a similar condition or with friends or family who is, this book is an invaluable resource. Dan not only describes the medical measures that have helped him but tells of the many family members and friends who have given him encouragement and strength to prevail against all odds. He has shown us how faith, hope, and love can empower us to do above and beyond what we thought possible. Dan had to step down from a distinguished career in education, but he forged on with his music and writing as he supports others facing similar health challenges. He is an exemplary husband, parent, and grandparent to a growing family. Read his story, and you will be inspired to walk on through whatever storms come your way. You will discover the secret power of gratitude, which Dan holds and freely shares with others."

—Reverend Dr. Jay Bartow, Retired Pastor
Emeritus
First Presbyterian Church of Monterey

"I have known Dan through our support group network for much of his journey with his mysterious neurological disorder. While many of his steps along the way have been frustrating and challenging, he always seems to find a positive outlook—one that inspires the rest of the group. I hope you get uplifted from his stories of challenge, acceptance and hope."

—Janet Edmunson, Author of *Finding Meaning with Charles*, Motivational Speaker, and CurePSP Support Group Facilitator

"Dan Brooks is a person of grace and wisdom. He writes movingly about his journey of neurological decline. Despite the symptoms that have been thrown his way over the last fifteen years and some unfortunate encounters with physicians, Dan's voice has not diminished. He openly shares his story as a way to help others on a similar path. By virtue of his constant adaptations to cope and even thrive, Dan is an inspiration to me and many others."

—Robin Riddle, CEO, Brain Support Network

FURTHER ALONG

Further Along

BY DAN R. BROOKS

Charleston, SC
www.PalmettoPublishing.com

Further Along
Copyright © 2021 by Dan R. Brooks

First Edition

ISBN: 978-1-63837-503-6

DEDICATION

This book is for Karrie and my dad. Karrie is the love of my life, my best friend, and the reason I am doing as well as I am fighting this disease process. She does so much for me and our whole nuclear family. Our dad, Ron "RC" Brooks, was a wonderful guitarist and a man of strong faith in Christ. He shared his life, his music, and his beliefs with his family, and we are all better for it. We will miss you and think of you always, Dad. RIP 10/3/29–10/7/20

CONTRIBUTIONS

Cover design by Stephen Brooks
Illustrations by Mark Brooks
Preface by Daniel Brooks, Jr.
Editing and Advisement by Karrie Brooks
Additional Editing by Jay Bartow
Endorsements by:
Janet Edmundson
Robin Riddle
Jay Bartow

TABLE OF CONTENTS

Preface xiii

Forward xv

1. My Questions Cut Like a Knife 1
2. Deep Brain Stimulation 25
3. Refined Diagnosis 41
4. Looking Back 51
5. Atypical Parkinsonism: Insidious and Elusive 65
6. Living on with Disease Progression 79
7. Tracheostomy and Feeding Tube 101
8. A New Normal 127
9. Faith and Mortality 137
10. Further Along 155
11. Gratitude 165

Acronyms, Terms, and Abbreviations 173

A Portrait 175

Preface

In the decade plus since my father wrote his first book, *I Will Go On: Living With a Movement Disorder*, so much has happened for Dad and for our family. The last year or so, in particular, has been eventful, to say the least. The global COVID-19 pandemic has changed life in so many ways, but the challenges of 2020 did not just start for us with the COVID pandemic. For Dad and the rest of our family, so much of the trouble of 2020 began in January, when Dad had a medical emergency. That story is recorded here in this book. Regardless of how you define words like miracle or miraculous, that Dad survived those events to tell his story here seems nothing short of miraculous to me. It is certainly not like anything I was expecting while waiting in the hall outside Dad's hospital room, comforting my mother, while the emergency-room doctor attempted to sedate and reintubate him en route to the ICU (where he spent a number of days). I'm so grateful that he made it, that he and Mom stayed safe during the pandemic, and that he intends to keep writing, playing music, and telling stories into the future.

Forward

As I begin again to write this account, I am reminded that I wrote my first book, *I Will Go On: Living with a Movement Disorder* (2009 BookSurge Publishing, later to become CreateSpace) to bring together the many posts written on PD Plus Me, a weblog. So much has occurred since the writing of that book, and further exploration is needed to share with you, my readers. This is due to several factors that are important to me:

1. There have been a number of important developments in the diagnosis of the specific atypical parkinsonism syndrome I have.

2. As we wove our way through the medical system, we encountered a number of institutions and individuals that have impacted my experience with a degenerative brain disease, both positively and negatively.

3. Deep brain stimulation surgery in 2012 has had a number of positive outcomes that should

be published for the benefit of all interested patients and their caregivers.

4. In January 2020 I had a breathing crisis which led to my life being saved by a tracheostomy and a PEG feeding tube, two outcomes of an atypical parkinsonism syndrome that are not uncommon occurrences, though these diseases themselves are rare in the broader context. This was a life-changing experience and I seek to write about those experiences to help others who may have the potential of facing the same issues.

5. The process of living out the effects of this disease has been one of growing and learning, leading to new ideas, perceptions and specific suggestions that I believe would be helpful to others encountering challenges, similar or otherwise.

I will invite the reader to go back and read my first book, and thus, I have given this second book the title *Further Along*. Reading my first book, though optional in order to appreciate this additional account, will give you perspective that will come from understanding the changes I have undergone as my diagnosis has been better defined and focused. If you prefer to start with this book, never fear that it will confuse the reading of *I Will Go On* at a later date.

This new book represents me today and thus will contain all the information you will need to get to know my journey and where I have traveled in the process. Everything about this book and the information in it is made complete and informed by the relationship I have with my wife and best friend, Karrie Brooks (born Magness), and all I am and have been able to do is in gratitude to her.

Dr. Wayne Brightman (an alias that I will use in reference to him—and I will do in kind concerning all other medical doctors that I refer to in order to maintain their anonymity) was the neurologist who originally made the clinical diagnosis of my condition. I began to experience neurological symptoms in 2005 and reported these to my primary care doctor that fall. I was initially referred to a neurologist who made a stab at the diagnosis and provided my first dosage of carbidopa/levodopa. This medication proved helpful, but in the first several visits I had with Dr. Thom Seemly, I did not establish a direction that was clarifying my condition in a specific manner. Karrie and I thought it best we move on, and we were referred to Dr. Wayne Brightman. Dr. Brightman was able to take the necessary steps to better focus on my condition.

Dr. Brightman ran several tests, including a PET scan that ruled out Alzheimer's disease, and sent me for magnetic resonance imaging examinations regularly for about six years, with one each year. He explained that I had significant brain atrophy and that he believed my case was most probably atypical parkinsonism. He had my blood evaluated for mad cow disease, Lou Gehrig's disease, and each time I saw him, he ran me through the physical examination of my movements and neurological issues that were observable. The fact that he was unsure of the exact syndrome was something he never seemed to get beyond, though he did describe verbally on many occasions that I had Shy-Drager, progressive supranuclear palsy, or striatonigral degeneration. These, of course, are all atypical parkinsonism syndromes, and since my presentation was unusual, he was comfortable writing on my insurance forms a description of my primary symptoms: "Probable Shy-Drager with abnormal movements, a gait disorder and mild dementia."

There is more detail about Dr. Brightman's diagnostic process in my first book, *I Will Go On*, but it is not a necessary read in order to appreciate the next part of my story, which involves the refining of my diagnosis. Along the way, you will see that I was not always given the best possible care, though Karrie worked hard to get me the best medical care possible and went through much effort to find experts that would be covered by insurance.

Note regarding people and places: The accounts in this book reflect my recollection of events. Depending on the story involved, some names, locations, and descriptive information have been changed to protect the privacy of those depicted. Any dialogue has been written from my memory.

CHAPTER ONE

My Questions Cut Like a Knife

As I begin, I would like to comment about the medical professionals that have been so wonderful in knowledge, dedication, and service. Karrie and I have been the beneficiaries of the services of great physicians, psychologists, nurses, respiratory therapists, physical therapists, speech therapists, medical assistants, office staff and hospital support staff. We have been particularly thankful for the primary care physicians and specialists who have helped to pinpoint issues to be addressed and made referrals for needed benefits. Our neurologists, in the long view, have been the saving grace through all that we have traversed. We are grateful, and in telling the stories that follow, I want to say that these represent anomalies in our experience with the medical profession during these fifteen years of traveling the journey with an atypical parkinsonism syndrome. There are two such experiences that I want to convey because, in the chronology of things, they occurred shortly after the writing of the 2009 book we published. Hopefully, other patients who had to go through similar circumstances and the resulting confusion, anger and frustration, will be reassured that you are not alone in your experiences. With that introduction, I begin to tell the following stories of disappointment found in this first chapter.

After getting the news of a degenerative brain disease diagnosis and learning to live a life with that hanging over our heads, we began to seek experts who could further define my condition. Why was I facing such a diagnosis and how it was that I came to face all that it entailed was something I would always wrestle with, as described in *I Will Go On*. Now, in 2010, five years after meeting Dr. Brightman, I was still seeking some answers.

Dr. Brightman was experiencing a medical crisis of his own and was absent from his practice for most of a year. During this year I was forced to consider where I might seek medical attention and treatment for my chronic, fatal condition. I had what seemed a fortuitous moment that opened up an unusual offer that was too good to be true. In our community group, the local Parkinson's support group, a special speaker was appearing, and we were in attendance. Her title was movement disorder specialist, newly installed to head a neurology clinic at the Arid Region Medical Center within an hour's drive of our home. She had a strong background and had achieved several credentials with impressive areas of specialization, which included diagnostic abilities regarding degenerative brain syndromes and conditions.

Her presentation focused on diagnosing Parkinson's disease and the value of a brain surgery known as deep brain stimulation. This emphasis notwithstanding, at the conclusion of her presentation in early 2010, she boldly approached me. As I sat in my wheelchair, Dr. Sheila Stackhouse stated that she had heard of me as the former leader of the local Parkinson's group and knew of my diagnosis. She wanted to offer a free opportunity to evaluate my condition and explained that it was being offered to me, in particular. Dr. Stackhouse said, "I see the dystonic tremor of your head, and I don't think your diagnosis of atypical parkinsonism is accurate. Come and see me. I can help you."

I was immediately struck by this moment as both hurtful and hopeful. Hurtful because someone was declaring my four-year diagnosis null and void, helpful because she was promising real help and answers. When Karrie returned from the restroom, I spoke to her and explained how this proud Dr. Stackhouse had approached me and, without hearing my story, told me that the diagnosis I had was wrong but that she was willing to give me free medical care.

We both felt emotional about this offer and spent time talking about it. It turned out that the offer was real, and the fact that our regular neurologist, Dr.

Brightman, was off on an extended medical leave meant that this opportunity could be explored without interfering with his treatment of my condition. Neurologists were becoming scarce at our clinic, so getting in to see one was at best a twice-yearly possibility. After much discussion and Karrie's investigation into how insurance factors would possibly play into this scenario—should this first free visit result in a continued treatment or diagnostic journey—we decided that we didn't have anything to lose. We made an appointment and confirmed over the phone that this first visit would be free of charge.

The first visit to see Dr. Stackhouse was enticingly warm and informative. She explained her intention was to evaluate me without explanation from any prior history of diagnosis and that she preferred to start from my story and her anecdotal notes of this conversation. She examined me and watched my movements of limbs, eyes, and my walking gait. She sat down with us and indicated that I had either a genetic disease, ataxia, multiple system atrophy, or an unusual case of Parkinson's, which if I had it, would benefit from deep brain stimulation surgery. She ordered a number of tests and demonstrated great interest and warmth. The thoroughness of her examination was initially a great demonstration of her genuine desire to get to the bottom of my brain disease and find the answers to the question that had changed our lives so dramatically. I had no idea how much this initial behavior was actually a mirage.

Dr. Stackhouse rescheduled me for a follow-up examination. Karrie went to work, changing my insurance carrier from SCAN to Blue Cross because this group covered the medical center we would be going to in order to see Dr. Stackhouse.

One thing must be noted about Dr. Stackhouse: she was very concerned about some form of exposure or vulnerability because she made us sign a waiver. This caught my attention because of my writing and blogging and the way I lived my life as an advocate for other patients with movement disorders and other fatal neurological diseases. The waiver made us promise to never post any information about my medical case and her treatment online on the world-wide web. I didn't have a problem signing this because I rationalized that anything I had done writing-wise that preceded this agreement was okay because it had been my choice up and until that point. I also felt that her reach was limited to my right to speak of my own experience, so any writing or interaction I would do on the internet after that moment would carefully exclude her name and the name of her organization. I was very careful to not violate that standard I set for myself. I came to realize that this safeguard would not be enough to keep her from reacting. Keep in mind, I had not initiated her examination, diagnosis, or treatment but had only gone to see her at her request.

The second appointment was as warm and friendly as the first. She asked me to come without my medication being taken that day, and we arrived fairly early in the morning without my usual tremor-fighting and body-stabilizing drug, carbidopa-levadopa (commonly known by the brand name Sinemet). She ran me through the usual battery of tests, including finger tapping, palm up/palm down patterns, rubbing my heal against my shin toward the floor on each leg, touching her finger and then reaching to point to my nose, observing my gait down the hall, walking in tandem and tapping my heal on the floor. There are several others, but these are among the group of commonly used Parkinson's disease tests. She was thinking that it would be important to establish whether I had idiopathic Parkinson's because her desire was to draw patients to the newly established movement disorder center, where she was the first neurologist hired to foster. Her aim, if this diagnosis was confirmed, would be the potential of deep brain stimulation surgery. It appeared to us she was thinking like a true scientist, and she directed us to have lunch and take the carbidopa/levodopa dose in the afternoon and rest while it would pass the blood brain barrier—then she would conduct the tests again to see how well I would respond to the medication.

After these steps, she returned to the examination room and ran the same battery of tests. She noted, as had Dr. Brightman four years earlier, that if I tried to walk in tandem (i.e., heal to toe in a straight line), I would easily fall over and have trouble even picking up a foot to place in front of the other without falling. She did the pull test from behind me, and I went back without any ability to right myself, just as I had without the medication administered.

She concluded that I was in need of physical therapy, several blood tests, and genetic testing to determine if I had a familial form of Parkinson's or ataxia, and she referred me to a neuropsychologist for a full battery of psychological tests. The doctor she referred me to—I will call her Dr. Cindy Synchronicity—seemed to be her go-to and was very reluctant to take my case, admitting that she, "Didn't have much experience examining patients with Parkinson's disease."

After a lot of persuading by Karrie, she was able to get a neuropsychological evaluation approved by the medical insurance. We went for an initial consultation and then scheduled a full Saturday testing day. It was a lot of work, with mental tests, physical tests, specific memory challenges, and an end-of-day true-and-false test that asked me a lot of strange questions that seemed designed more to find a mental disorder than to help determine which neurodegenerative disease I had.

After this information was completed, Dr. Synchronicity called to let us know she wanted to have an appointment to talk with us, indicating that she felt that there was a psychological condition that she seemed predetermined to use as an explanation for the atypical parkinsonism syndrome I presented.

We had all the blood work done, and I had none of the genetic or other disease processes that would cause the brain disorder that Dr. Brightman had diagnosed as atypical parkinsonism. He had done all of the supportive studies and had observed me for four years. The physical therapists at Arid Region Medical Center were making progress in both physical and occupational therapy. The exercises and activities were giving me a lot of help. I felt that this observable walking data could be reported to Dr. Stackhouse to assist in her complete evaluation. I suggested that the therapist give her a call and let her know the issues she saw me having with walking, the balance struggles I had exhibited for years, and my hand-eye coordination problems that they were working on—all related to the degenerative brain disease process I was living with that had taken my career from me and had affected my loved ones, who care so much.

The next time we went to see Dr. Stackhouse, she was literally like a different doctor. I, to this day, have no way of knowing what the neuropsychologist, Dr. Synchronicity, had said about me, which I felt must have been a misperception on her part, given her limited experience with an atypical parkinsonism patient. Or perhaps Dr. Stackhouse was angry with me when she found that I had a blog online and had published an autobiographical book about my challenges. The only thing I know is that she wanted to cut me loose and said, "What else have you been doing that you haven't told me?"

I said, "What do you mean?"

She seemed to allude to my participation in support groups, my online story, and my attempt to "keep on keeping on" with my life, in spite of my challenges. She said, "I can't do anything for you. It is not Parkinson's disease, and I think you should see Dr. Synchronicity to work on your issues."

I was dumbfounded. Having been a patient of a distinguished neurologist who had been on medical leave simultaneously with Dr. Stackhouse's visit to our local Parkinson's support group, I knew that I had an extrapyramidal disorder due to a degenerative brain disease, and it caused the atypical parkinsonism syndrome. She was now denying this fact, assuming it was farcical and showing disdain for my suffering. Karrie was so angry that, when the doctor walked out of the door to get my paperwork together, she said aloud, "Let's get out of this place!"

I love how Karrie always fights for me and is my best advocate.

This so-called specialist had walked up to me and told me my diagnosis was wrong and offered me an initial visit for free. She sought me out because I had been the group leader and had a lot of experience within the Parkinson's community, and she saw me as a mark to bring others to their clinic. I hadn't asked for this trouble, but I realized her paranoia was the issue along with her fear of being exposed for some reason, because she had asked me initially to sign away my personal right to express myself online. I had carefully not written on my blog, We Will Go On, anything specific about my neurological treatment and never gave a name of a clinic or physician, but she was seemingly angry or disillusioned by my involvement in her world. She left her post at this hospital soon after, taking a position in a completely different region of the country. I have never publicly spoken of this and feel relieved to write about it here in this book. Now, other patients who experience problems with doctors, which are few and far between, can read this account and have a chance to say, "That problem with the doctor wasn't me, was it?" and "That specialist didn't know what she was seeing," even though another movement disorder specialist would figure it out for them.

The next thing I did when we arrived home was call Dr. Synchronicity. I said to her, "Do not write about me, send anyone a report, or discuss my medical records with anyone ever again."

I put the same in writing and mailed it to her. I wrote to Dr. Stackhouse and directed her to seal my file and say nothing to anyone or send any information out to any clinic or doctor at any time in the future. She never acknowledged my request or agreed to do as I had asked. That chapter ended, but before my original neurologist, Dr. Brightman, was able to return, I would have one more disappointing experience with a renowned neurologist who seemed to have heard from Dr. Stackhouse.

There are a lot of factors that come into play in these situations, which include profit motives, ego drives, and personality issues that a small percentage of physicians have the potential to develop. Looking back, I realize that it was our mistake to take Dr. Stackhouse up on her offer, and I was grateful for the attempt, especially when she began at my first visit by acknowledging that I had the very syndrome Dr. Brightman had diagnosed: atypical parkinsonism and, more specifically, multiple system atrophy. Apparently, this all disappeared with her fear of my knowledge of my own condition and my many contacts. The neuropsychologist had misread me, and having little or no experience with neurodegenerative diseases, she did not know what she was seeing symptomatically. I felt hurt, disgusted, and angry. It was a long ride home when we left that arid climate and headed home with our heads down, knowing that we had wasted time and treasure for an empty and painful feeling that left me feeling attacked.

I was fortunate to have met a well-known neurologist at a regional state university I will call University of Ivy Halls. He was a friendly individual—if somewhat quiet in nature—whom I had met at the first support group we attended in a nearby county, closer to the coast. He was the head of a department of neurology and provided oversight for a group that we were invited to join by a professional contact I had as an assistant superintendent before my retirement. In early 2006, we met Dr. Wisenstein, a neurologist who specialized in the study and treatment of Parkinson's and other related diseases.

I attended this group for a bit over two years and went to several events and group meetings, which included discussions between patients with guidance from Dr. Wisenstein. Dr. Wisenstein and I sat beside one another at a potluck or two and found that we had common interests in a couple of areas, including guitars and music. I felt that we had been friendly on several occasions and that he knew me as an acquaintance. Secondly, we had attended a second group for atypical parkinsonism syndromes at the University of Ivy Halls, where he again was sponsoring a group and providing a modicum of guidance for its leaders. This put the time I had come across Dr. Wisenstein and his two groups he supported at a period of four years.

After striking out with Dr. Stackhouse, I was still very interested in having an expert interpret my long list of symptoms that had led to my atypical parkinsonism syndrome diagnosis. We determined that a cash payment would be needed due to the fact my insurance would not cover this examination, and Karrie wanted to commit those dollars to getting the answers we both wanted and needed. We scheduled an appointment, and when it was rescheduled at the request of

Dr. Wisenstein for late on a Friday afternoon, we realized this would be an arduous drive from Riverside to the University of Ivy Halls near the coast. Knowing the great amount of traffic that would be on the freeway at rush hour on a Friday evening in Southern California, we felt that this changed appointment time was very much intended to give us the desire to cancel.

When Dr. Wisenstein entered the examination room, it was apparent that he had no intention of actually testing me thoroughly enough to determine what specific form of parkinsonism I had. He seemed to feign that he didn't know me from those hours we had spent in each other's presence at several events over a four-year period, and he stopped short of giving me any kind of thorough examination. My disease causes serious walking issues, and all neurologists have me walk back and forth to get a sense of the difficulty and to determine what it might indicate. He did not do such a test, an example of a number of movement tests he did not conduct with me. He seemed vague, and the implication from our visit was that he had never met me, and he concluded he had no idea what I had—whether progressive supranuclear palsy, multiple system atrophy, or corticobasal syndrome, some conditions under consideration in my case.

I left feeling that I had been stabbed in the back and wondered how Dr. Wisenstein had come to see me as unworthy of a complete diagnosis for my $400. I had thought of him as a friend to the Parkinson's community, to which I belonged, and I'd had confidence in his ability to diagnose such conditions. "He simply," as my wife Karrie put it, "did not come to play." She added that, "Based on what tests he did not run on you and what he didn't ask, he had determined in advance he had no intention of providing a diagnosis."

On September 24, 2011, the day after seeing Dr. Wisenstein and experiencing his pretense, I was very upset and thought it best to write a letter to my wife. This was a way to get this on paper and also provide an outlet for my feelings which I knew were problematic to share publicly. Now that nine years have passed and I have had a confirmed diagnosis from several excellent neurologists, I am sharing this story in my book. You will be among the first to read it. Here is the letter I penned to Karrie the Saturday morning following this examination:

September 24, 2011
Dearest Karrie,

I have such deep feelings this morning and am unable to effectively express them in audible words. I need to write my feelings down on paper, which of necessity, ironically, I must type if I am going to be able to write it legibly, and without severe cramping in my hand that I get when I try to write anything in long hand of any serious length. Please allow me to tell you what is going through my mind regarding yesterday's visit with Dr. Wisenstein (I will henceforth refer to him as Dr. W).

I am concerned this morning because I believe I have been diagnosed inaccurately by Dr. W. I know that he did not state that I do not have a serious neurological disorder, or that he indicated that he thinks I don't suffer with this. I must admit though, on that point, that he didn't give the impression that he could tell, from what I was able to say, that I am in pain. My condition is so severe to live with, as you know, that it is hard to be told that it is an ambiguous disorder or condition. I find it incredible that it has so little outward manifestations that is indistinguishable. I am just broken hearted by the frustration of having a world renowned movement disorder specialist spend a half hour with me, just to say he can't tell what I have.

Somewhere in the dyskinesia or chorea movements, or both, he was unable to determine that I have tremors. When I woke this morning with the trembling in my body, particularly my chest, neck, and head, I was angry that he was obviously unable to believe or detect it. By the way, I am not angry at him personally, but myself, for my scattered way of telling him about my experience. I don't think he saw or heard what he needed to, and as you said, "Dan, you do benefit from carbidopa/levodopa," and you were absolutely correct. This is one area that I failed to properly tell him, although I had the feeling during the exam, and particularly this morning, that I was none too convincing about anything I am experiencing.

In my opinion, he didn't get that I was disabled. He indicated that he didn't have the impression that I was necessarily unable to drive or work. This isn't an absolute judgement of his thoughts, and I don't mean to read into his reaction. I am only stating that it was my impression that he was looking at me as if to say, "And why did you retire when you did? You didn't have a proper diagnosis." I would like to say, "It wasn't as a result of a particular diagnosis that led to my being rendered disabled, but rather the serious neurological condition I had then, and have more so now, that made continuing impossible." Here again, I am not taking it personally that he couldn't receive that fact. I only think that it was hard to tell him the essential problems and struggles I have because of what seemed to be a rush to judgement on his part that my atypical neurological condition didn't fit any of what he considered his appropriate columns or categories.

To be the person I am today, having experienced what I have, and to have the hope of a movement disorder specialist's diagnostic wisdom bestowed on me, I am deeply disappointed. You did everything you could to not allow me to set myself up for this reaction, and I am working hard this morning to be brave and positive about my situation, but I can't pretend it is not a very painful moment in my life. This was at best a very good opportunity to realize that, in the difficulty Dr. Brightman has had pinpointing my diagnosis, he has been quite right in labeling it an extrapyramidal syndrome and an abnormal involuntary movement disorder of an organic nature. Dr. W's apparent bewilderment about my condition confirms the validity of Dr. Brightman's words, and in that sense, it did provide reinforcement for the fact that I am a very unique and "bizarre" case. These are truths that you helped me to cement in my mind as we sat together last night and ate dinner. That debriefing with you did help because I was able to understand better what had taken place.

Hearing again from a doctor that the complicated nature of my condition is confusing and difficult to read is also a matter of great disappointment to me. I feel so aware of the many parkinsonian, abnormal cognitive, and ataxia related symptoms that I have to go through and deal with every hour of every day that it makes me want to cry. I am deeply disappointed that I was not able—in my one shining moment—to make these symptoms evident to such an important specialist as Dr. W. I feel that I am living so alone with my tremors, stiffness, imbalance, unclear thoughts, facial masking, loss of strength in my limbs, musculoskeletal pain, eye movement restrictions, digestive problems, urinary dysfunction, and struggle to walk that I am on the verge of giving up hope of ever knowing anything, truly, from a medical standpoint. I am crestfallen by that reality.

As a thinking person, I honestly believe that some of this is a badly timed train wreck. Had I been sitting in Dr. W's office six years ago, and had he been taking me through this diagnostic process, he would have over time realized exactly what Dr. Brightman has known for years now—I have an extrapyramidal disorder, and it is very real and organic in nature. Dr. Brightman has diagnosed me as having a Parkinsonism-plus disorder and has stated so on several occasions. I am quite sure that he is right, but I feel so much upheaval this morning that I am unable to sustain any confidence in anything, right at the moment.

I am trying to remain objective, but it can't be hard to understand how I might feel both despair and embarrassment, too, however different those two words are. It is difficult to realize that I could be with and around Dr. W. and the two support groups in which he is involved, only to find out that he has had the impression that I was on the wrong diagnosis road through these last five and a half years that he has casually observed me (I realize that it is unfair to characterize his observation as anything specific or intentional, but humor me for the sake of my attempting to define my feelings).

It is either that, or last night when I was in his office, he should have discussed my tremors with me and the relief that I do or don't have from Sinemet. I needed to have an opportunity for him to observe my walking gait, and I am truly shocked that he didn't follow that protocol. Also, the "pull test" for balance would have made sense. These are just meant as examples of tests I am aware are used for such a diagnosis. I can't help but think that the fantastic nature of my movements and the sense of unusualness of my story fell on skeptical ears.

I am tired of doctors such as Dr. Stackhouse and Dr. W giving this kind of response. As I began, I am truly suffering and do not feel I am believable in the most essential ways. I have tremors—all through my body—and yet because it isn't isolated to a single hand, I am treated with skepticism. This is getting older all the time. I have eye movement difficulties and abnormalities, as noted by two opthamologists. This is obviously a brain connected issue, but somehow my speech struggles, coordination problems, and eye issues do not point to the very diseases that describe just those symptoms.

I didn't bring up Parkinsonism-plus. Dr. Brightman did, and I think he did so for very good reasons. Somehow, because I am not known to these other doctors, I am not completely believable. I am not implying that they don't think I am a trustworthy person but rather that I think they are viewing me as having a phenomenon of my own misperceived medical difficulties. This impression is one of the reasons I began by saying, "I am broken hearted." I am hurt really because I have my feet firmly on the ground in the sense that I know what I know I am feeling and experiencing. Because it is compounded and doesn't fit neatly into a small enough box, known as "X" disease, it creates a skeptical reaction.

I sincerely appreciate the opportunity you made possible for me to have this alternate opinion. I thank you for all of the work, love, and hope that you put into this. I know I will get a better view of this whole picture as time passes and I am able to step away from the emotion and pain it has inadvertently caused, but for right now, I am a bit myopic and am seeing some of the downsides of the issue.

I appreciate the clarification at dinner that Dr. W. had no prejudice toward me and didn't come off as being predisposed to a hasty misinterpretation of my condition. I think that this circumstance was a perfect train wreck caused by the varied nature and complexity of my symptoms. As a result, Dr. W. honestly didn't have a quality viewpoint that he cared to share other than "I am sorry I can't be more specific or clear for you. I just simply don't know at this point." I am glad you reinforced that he recommended that a neuro-ophthalmologist examine me. That does tend to indicate he recognizes there is a serious neurological issue.

I do go on with my life with questions. A key concern is "Why does my having one of the more overt and complicated movement disorders mean I get less information, am treated as having less credibility, and, as a result, receive less support than if I had a more easily diagnosed condition?" For five and a half years (we first went to a support group in January of 2006) I have had to be the one on the outside looking in as I viewed others who had milder movement disorder symptoms. Dr. Brightman has said on numerous occasions, "I can't simply call this Parkinson's as others have because it is so much more." If it is so much more—and boy, does it seem apparent to me mentally and physically—why are specialists so afraid to say that they see some specific symptoms? Maybe chorea, eye movements, and balance problems like mine are much rarer than typical Parkinson's disease and thus are even harder to make a call on for the likes of a movement disorder specialist? I am beginning to seriously ponder that this is the case. At this moment, with the areas of uniqueness found in my condition, I do doubt any doctor's ability to assess and detect these nuanced issues. I can't come to any other conclusion, since I am experiencing the reality of these manifestations.

I wanted to be able to get as much of my thinking down on paper as I could while it was swirling, freshly in my mind and heart. These are not final conclusions, but they are seriously considered musings that I am intending as sincere, if not a bit skewed by my mood and subjective position. Please know that I am continuing to view myself as being an overcomer, and I will go on, despite this very disappointing set of circumstances. I do not want to call this examination a mistake because I know I will learn some valuable things from it—about both my disease and my own areas of growth that will result. I will keep on believing there are answers and remedies out there in the future. I will keep on playing and singing, reading, laughing, and loving each and every day I am fortunate to spend with you, my favorite person.

Thank you for reading my thoughts and for being the one I can count on to believe me when I share my perspective about my medical challenges with you. I am so grateful that I have always had you to believe and care about what is happening in my mind and body. It means so much that you are able to be so objective, sincere, and loving through all of these brave attempts to find the answers we so desperately need. You handle all this so well, and I know that you are deeply hurt by the pain I am experiencing, too. I know how much you care, and I know it is something that you would give anything to fix or change for me.

How could we not try one more time to get more defi-nite answers? Well, we did, and I owe that to you. I thank you and love you for all the ways you give and support me. You are the best and I love you with all my heart.

Love always,

Dan

It was my desire to have a second opinion, and during Dr. Brightman's absence, I was drawn to be seen by this distinguished doctor who was considered an expert in movement disorders. The fact that I had an atypical parkinsonism syndrome he hadn't denied; he simply refused to participate in the opinion because of what he perceived as my desire to keep his opinion private. I felt that I had the right to do it without re-leasing Dr. Wisenstein's findings to any other physician initially because I wanted time to consider the meaning of a diagnosis from such an expert in his field. Having known him as a sponsor of two of our support groups and having had personal conversations with him about guitars and Parkinson's disease while eating potlucks and drinking coffee, I was sure he would treat me fairly.

I already had one of the best neurologists in the country take all the necessary steps to figure out that I had a neurodegenerative disease that caused abnormal movements, but the lack of specificity was bothering me. Once Dr. Stackhouse opened that door and stuck her foot in it, I was longing to know where I fit and how I might belong somewhere. There are different support groups for each of the atypical parkinsonism disorders. Now that I have had the diagnosis of Dr. Nancy Holcomb (as I will discuss later) to support Dr. Brightman's decision about the label, I am comfortable with the knowledge of what has stolen my wellness from me. Nevertheless, I won't ever completely get over what Dr. Stackhouse and Dr. Wisenstein took from me by showing disinterest or disdain for my or my dear wife's feelings and concerns.

CHAPTER 2

Deep Brain Stimulation

Having unsuccessfully attempted to get a second opinion, or a third for that matter, I was disappointed to realize that there was no neurologist as honest and willing to help me as Dr. Brightman. Dr. Brightman had recovered from his own medical crisis and was now back at our clinic and available to continue seeing me. He had been right all long and was still sticking to his atypical parkinsonism diagnosis. In early 2012, he sat down with Karrie and me, after a thorough yearly examination, and said there is a syndrome called striatal nigral degeneration. This was defined better as the parkinsonian version of the atypical parkinsonism syndromes, or atypical parkinsonian disorders. Striatal nigral degeneration—or "SND"—takes the form of parkinsonism, with the symptoms of Parkinson's disease: tremor, rigidity, slowness of movement, and balance trouble. Added to these are autonomic troubles, speech, swallowing and eye movement difficulty. SND is now known as MSA-P—or multiple system atrophy, parkinsonian-type.

He went on to suggest that I take time to consider DBS (deep brain stimulation) surgery, for which he would refer me to a neurosurgeon who was an expert in that procedure. I agreed to think it over and soon after made the appointment to see Dr. Merrill Morgan. We had a consultation and discussed whether I would be a good candidate. Dr. Morgan thought that I would be an excellent candidate and also that this surgery could improve my quality of life and potentially extend my life.

Karrie and I discussed it, talked to our adult children, and decided that, at the age of fifty-six, I would have the surgery. First, there would need to be additional tests, which included being videotaped while walking, conducting movements of my limbs, and speech production. I was videoed while writing with a pen, making a spiral. All of this demonstrated various actions that were important to document why the surgery was recommended for my particular degenerative brain disorder.

The surgery would be conducted in a large community hospital and would involve three major steps. First, the insertion of guide screws; second, the surgical implant of probes within my brain; and third, another surgical event, which would involve the implantation of a generator device that would be connected to the two implants in my deep brain near my basal ganglia, the movement center.

First, I had an appointment in early July of 2012 to have eight screws put into my skull. This was done in Dr. Morgan's offices. Karrie and our son, Daniel, came with me to this appointment. I was fairly nervous about this event. After screws were put it, I would go downstairs to have a CT scan to provide a map of my brain that would be used to locate the exact placement of the two probes to be inserted into my brain. Daniel and Karrie wished me well as I went into the office to have the procedure. I had the eight places on my scalp anesthetized locally with a needle. This took a lot of pressure on the top of my scalp from Dr. Morgan, who did it with great care and precision. Nonetheless, he had to press down hard on my head as he went through the thin layer of tissue and muscle that is under the skin on our heads. He pushed with great force, eight times, to get the needle through and released the pain-numbing agent into my scalp. It worked well, although this was a painful and fear producing process.

Following the local anesthesia, the eight screws were inserted. This was painless. The screwdriver was quiet and efficient, like a high-tech cordless screwdriver that a surgeon would use. He put in what I believe were titanium screws, and I felt the vibration as they cut into the skull bone eight times to thread their way to a firm attachment. When this was done, I joked that I looked like the movie character Hellraiser, with the eight pins sticking out from my skull. They were spread out in a geometric pattern in order to make a grid of my brain on a computer that would create crosshairs to be used for the two probes to be placed deep in my brain. Each probe tip would be implanted in just the right location to provide the most accurate placement to help stem the movement issues caused by faulty signals in my basal ganglia.

I was sent downstairs with these screws in place, causing a bit of blood to seep from several that were visible to me from the front as I peered in the mirror. I was to have the CT images taken, which wasn't a long procedure. I remember the imaging professional telling me that her husband was a fellow Parkinson's disease patient that I actually had known. He too had DBS surgery with the surgeon, Dr. Morgan. She told us about her husband's progress and how the surgery had benefited him. Karrie and I were both reassured by the words of this nice lady conducting my scan.

I went home to sleep with these small, silvery-white screws sticking out of my head, knowing I would rise early in the morning to get ready to go to the hospital. I think I was scheduled for somewhere around 8:30 a.m., but I was to be at the hospital by 6:00 a.m. I was taken down to the pre-op area with Karrie. Our sons, Daniel, Mark, and Stephen, visited before the surgery started, as did our Pastor Brad Copeland, who prayed with me for my wellbeing and the outcome of the surgery.

Soon, I was inside the operating room. My friendly, knowledgeable surgeon had told our son Mark prior to my operation that "God guides my hands, and I follow His directions implicitly." He showed us my CT image with map-like crossing lines at ninety-degree angles and told us that he would place the probes within the range of a single grain of rice of the targets. Right after the surgery was completed, I had a CT scan and returned to the recovery area, where Daniel came to see how I was doing. Dr. Morgan came in to review the results with us and showed Daniel the overlay of CT scans on his smart phone, one depicting the image of my brain prior to surgery and the other from after surgery, matched up. The placement of the probes was exact!

I came from the recovery room to greet my sons, Daniel, Mark and Stephen and my wife, Karrie, in the hallway. They were thrilled that I was awake and feeling well. I had a number of family and friends who all came in my room after I arrived in the intensive care unit for the day and night I would stay in the hospital. I did well, though I did vomit one time or two, fairly violently, which wasn't abnormal for brain surgery patients to experience. The next morning I told my registered nurse that I wasn't ready to go home. I felt it was hard to put my feet down on the floor, as the left one kept tapping up and down involuntarily, and I was still nauseous. My surgeon knew better and said I would be fine at home.

We arrived home to a small grasslands fire in the little valley behind our home. This was a detail I logged mentally right away. I had the hiccups, which required a call to the surgeon to get an anti-nausea drug that my surgeon prescribed. I remember well that the first couple of nights my scalp hurt badly. It seemed I had pain in my head, not deeply, but on the surface and in the tissue just below the scalp. It was very painful that first few days. This made sense, considering nickel-sized holes had to be drilled though my skull in two places. I was taking Norco in a medium dose on a regular basis for a week or so.

More importantly, I remember our sons (young adult men, with two already married at that time, the youngest in a serious relationship with a young lady that he would eventually marry) coming to the house to visit a few minutes. I was able to stand up straight and tall and walk with less trouble. The jerky, repetitive tremor of my neck and head was almost nonexistent. The surgery appeared to have worked very well! I was excited. I was experiencing the benefits of the DBS surgery, and I didn't yet have the generator that sends the signals from my chest to my brain implanted.

From the surgery on Thursday morning until the following Tuesday morning, I was able to experience what felt like a honeymoon from my symptoms of jerky movements and difficulty standing up straight. My spine would normally pull my head forward and bend my shoulders downward in a curved posture.

During these early days, that posture disappeared. This, we were told, was the result of the insertion of the probes in those locations of the brain that affect and control movements. Merely surgically placing them in those locations near the left and right side of the subthalamic nuclei had stimulated these areas, interrupting the bad signals going to my extremities that normally malfunctioned.

The following Tuesday morning, the generator surgery was more routine. The generator was surgically implanted in the upper right portion of my chest, and the leads from that were then connected or plugged into the wires that were bundled just above my collar bone. During the implant surgery the week before, the probes were inserted into two nickel-sized holes drilled in the top of my head, five inches or so back from my forehead. The wires were then capped in the holes with what I light-heartedly refer to as manhole covers, like you would find on the street. These were permanently glued in place, and extra wire was coiled beneath my scalp to prevent problems from pulling that would dislodge the probes. The wires were bundled under my scalp and were channeled behind my right ear, under the skin on the right side of my neck under the ear. This wire bundle, about one-fourth an inch in diameter, appears like a large vessel that arches over my collar bone and down under my skin where it meets the generator. This is what was connected in the second surgery that Tuesday morning. The generator contains a battery that has now been replaced twice, with four years between each replacement. The average lifespan of these generator batteries is five years.

The DBS generator provides a steady stream of low-current electricity that is sent into the movement control center of my brain and provides a blocking action to prevent the harmful signals heading to my body that cause abnormal movements such as trouble walking, speaking, and jerky tremors or shaking. Overall, I had a very positive outcome from this surgery, and I experienced better days. It wasn't perfect, and there were some symptoms that persisted and others that were side effects. Emotional feelings that are hard to contain are known phenomena in the wake of such a surgery. The following event took place within the next year, following my deep brain stimulation surgery.

Eight weeks after I had a double implant DBS surgery, I reflected on the impact of this life-changing process. Literally, I had two surgeries, one to receive the bilateral implant, and four days later, I was back to have the wires and generator installed, which is similar to a pacemaker. The wires were placed under my scalp and inside the skin on my neck, while the generator was placed in my upper chest. This has been a very helpful and beneficial procedure. I have reduced tremors, much less dyskinesia, and an improved ability to walk, and my voice has improved in strength and clarity.

This is brain surgery, nonetheless, and it is no walk in the park. With all the good involved, what things are the most challenging about DBS, one could ask? I would start with the fact that you need to be prepared for a time of respite to recover. It is important to rest and not strain. There are scalp muscles involved in the surgery, and these tissues are engaged as we turn our heads, lift objects, or make facial expressions. I had forty-six staples, and those were holding down my scalp for most of two weeks.

Once the staples are removed, the head still needs to recover and this takes well over a month, in my experience. Be patient. The two entry points to put the leads into my brain were sore for three to four weeks. It was like a very bad headache at times, and it is important to realize that these are manageable if you don't overreact. The tendency is to think that the pain may be a bigger problem, though in my case, it never was. I took two extra-strength Tylenol and tried to relax.

I desired to get going soon after the surgery because, as in my case, I was moving so much better, I wanted to get into the yard, start exercising and play my guitars. Starting slowly and not trying to transition to these activities too quickly was important for me. I am sure each surgeon gives good direction to his/her patients regarding what they can begin to do and when. The other issue I ran across was getting used to the wires under the skin on my head and neck. The wires tug and feel strange at times. The pacemaker (generator device) is also something to get used to, both physically and psychologically. At times I was a bit depressed about having this hardware inside my body. It made me feel as though I had changed and would never be the same. When I went through these thoughts, I reminded myself of the tremendous benefits DBS brought me and that these electronics under my skin were a small price to pay for the joy of an improved life and renewed abilities. During those first weeks, I adjusted well to the implant surgery.

DBS is brain surgery, and it is a great opportunity, but it comes with several challenges. I was prepared for these because I took a couple of years to think about having the surgery before deciding to go forward. Also, my wife bought me a very good book, and we read it the month before. It is entitled *Life with a Battery-Operated Brain*, and it was written by Jackie Hunt Christensen. The author, who also has had bilateral DBS, does a great job of explaining the pros and cons, along with the details and facts about the devices involved and her personal surgery experiences.

I went into the surgery with my eyes open and fully aware of the variables involved. Ultimately, I had a *great* surgeon, and he not only knew what he was doing, but he discussed it thoroughly with me beforehand. He reminded me that DBS is not a cure but a treatment that improves one's quality of life. I have had many years of happiness because of my improved physical abilities.

It has been nine years since my brain surgery. When I consider the alternatives and the benefits that resulted, I would do it all again. Deep brain stimulation surgery was risky and, you could argue, ill-advised. Let me rephrase. It was generally thought that an atypical parkinsonism patient was not a good candidate for this procedure. However, I had the best neurosurgeon on earth. I really believe that. I trusted him and understood his ability and experience level. He explained the risk of a bleed and possible death, but he also told me that I had the chance of extending my life and giving myself a better quality of life to share with my most important priority above all priorities: my wonderful wife, Karrie, my fantastic sons, their wonderful spouses, and our five (going on six) beautiful grandkids! Wow, am I a wealthy man in all the right ways—referring to the people in my life. I am a simple man with simple values. My brain disease has changed all of my individual talents and practical abilities, as well as access to my career and mobility. I miss driving, working, leading, teaching, and organizing people. However, what really counts is one's quality of life.

Deep brain-stimulation surgery put implants in my brain and chest, along with cables in my neck, which enabled me to make larger movements with my limbs and keep moving better than I would have, for a much longer time. I have already gotten my money's worth. It has helped me for nine years, and it didn't do what the naysayers said it would—it didn't kill me in a year, as had occurred in the case of two individuals that I read about who had atypical parkinsonism syndrome and died within the first year of surgery. I learned while earning my educational doctorate degree that statistical significance goes up with the number of subjects and the controlling of variables. This was too small a sample size and over generalized, as far as I can determine.

My surgeon knows the brain and knew that I had an unusual case with many abnormal involuntary movement issues. This surgery didn't cure my disease. I still have a degenerative process progressing and now have more specifics about my diagnosis. I have corticobasal syndrome and multiple system atrophy. I am confident in my movement disorder specialist, who has done such a thorough job of assessing my symptoms and providing the best possible treatment. What a great doc! Also, going back, I originally had such a wonderful neurologist, Dr. Brightman, who took care of me for ten years, and recommended that I be evaluated for DBS. My primary care physician, Dr. Diane Hope, is wonderful and manages my case and all the variables. She is very responsive to all requests for specialists referrals and medical equipment. The specialists I have that treat me for breathing, swallowing, speech, cardiac, urinary, and digestive troubles all play a big role.

I am blessed. I am here, and my family surrounds me. We have a great church and loving friends all over. I would do it again. As I wrote in my song, "I Will Go On,"

As I contemplate I know the hour is late
I can't even find my heart
I lost it somewhere between the sky and the chair
I want to search; I just can't start
I'm writing these lines on this guitar of mine
Hoping I can find a way
To record the joy that I found one day
Over this emptiness it just won't stay.

And I will go on, walking on my way
And I'll sing my song
Though this emptiness gets in my way
But this loneliness just won't stay.

Yesterday, I couldn't find my way
These voices inside my room
They kept calling my name, it didn't sound the same
While looking out from my gloom
But I know that I just can't rely, on
seeing things from my view
Grasping in pain, at these bitter remains
And this loneliness can't get in my way.

And I will go on, walking on my way
And I'll sing my song
Though this emptiness gets in my way
But this loneliness just won't stay.

Though now I can find my way
And this emptiness just wouldn't stay.

From the album, I Will Go On (C) 2006
Dan Ryan Brooks Music, BMI

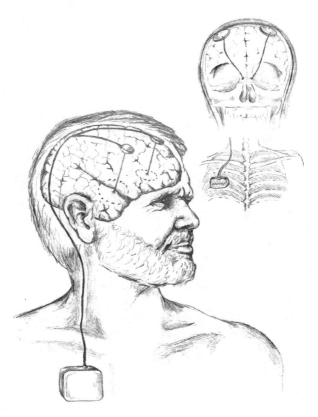

Deep Brain Stimulation Implants
with the Generator/Pacemaker in the Chest

CHAPTER 3

Refined Diagnosis

In 2016 a new opportunity for clarity of my diagnosis became possible.

First of all, I am very grateful to our great doctors: our primary care doctor at the clinic, the various specialists who treat me for everything from choking/swallowing difficulty to severe eye pain—and up to and including the outstanding movement disorder specialist/neurologist that is working so hard to find answers to my rare parkinsonian disorder.

For years, I wrote on my blog (since 2006 with some breaks) details of my experiences, feelings, faith struggles, spiritual plateaus, and thorough verbal descriptions that defined and categorized all of the various atypical parkinsonism syndromes that I am familiar with, if not experiencing. Most were a part of the first book I wrote, entitled *I Will Go On*. Most of you that are reading this are familiar with that volume.

Now, after all these years, I am at peace. I have for years been defined as having parkinsonism and one of the atypical parkinsonism syndromes, most likely Shy-Drager. Shy-Drager is known as multiple system atrophy, and I have the hallmark symptom, low blood pressure upon rising from bed or getting up from a sitting posture. This causes blacking out, loss of oxygen to the head, and it can be an hours-long condition where my neck and shoulders ache, my arms and upper extremities get a numbness and lack of feeling, and my strength is very limited, causing great fatigue. This blood pressure issue gives pause to my neurologist and is the reason why, in addition to corticobasal syndrome and parkinsonism (tremors, stiffness, loss of balance, and many other symptoms), Doctors think I also have MSA. This dual condition is now being referred to as a mixed pathology. This means that the proteins that develop abnormal degeneration are normally associated with one disease or another. Tau is a protein associated with corticobasal syndrome, and alpha synuclein breaks down to cause multiple system atrophy. I have destruction of both proteins, causing the conditions with which I have been diagnosed. It is rare to have corticobasal syndrome or multiple system atrophy, but it is very rare to have a mixed pathology. In saying this, though, my neurologist, Dr. Nancy Holcomb, says they are seeing this more often and are referring to a condition like mine in this way.

I respect my physicians and want to give them the space and freedom to consider all the avenues and pursue the best truth that leads to the best possible treatments. My deep brain stimulator is working for me and keeps me walking—at least enough to use my walker.

Karrie takes me on very nice outings to places such as Ikea or guitar stores. These short vacations require my wheelchair and mean that I have to dodge nice people all day long. It is always great to be out and part of the world for a time. Just enough time to let it sink in again—I may be disabled, but I am not grounded. Not completely. I have coricobasal syndrome: a loss of cells in my basal ganglia on both sides, enough to show up in my DaT scan results and cause the loss of body control that has put me in a walker and stolen my career.

After getting a better picture of my diagnosis, I began to want to write again, the impetus to write this very book. Meanwhile, I feel that I've got so much to do with my life. I'm a father, a husband, a grandpa with five (going on six) grandchildren, and a guitar and mandolin player! Life is beautiful!

Let me be more specific about the two conditions with which I have been diagnosed. When our local clinic was still seeking a permanent replacement for the retired Dr. Brightman, I was referred by my primary care physician, Dr. Diane Hope, to a movement disorder specialist, Dr. Nancy Holcomb, an outstanding neurologist at the Valley Arms University Medical Center, to get a very specific diagnosis. I was considered, as I had been for eleven years, as having atypical parkinsonism, with MSA, PSP and CBD all manifesting symptoms in my case. (Multiple system atrophy, progressive supranuclear palsy, and corticobasal degeneration). Now that I have been diagnosed with CBS and MSA, I would like to explain my layperson's understanding of these conditions.

CBD is often referred to as CBS (corticobasal syndrome) during life and confirmed as CBD after death. CBS is under the umbrella of atypical parkinsonism and, more specifically, one of the frontotemporal dementias (FTD). There are several categories under FTD, including PSP, CBS, and primary progressive aphasia (predominantly a severe language issue).

In my book *I Will Go On: Living with a Movement Disorder*, I discussed CBD, MSA, and PSP, knowing that I had the potential for being defined has having one of the three. I didn't know that, eleven years after publishing that book, my diagnosis would be possibly redefined. Well, that isn't the best way to express it: *further* defined is a more accurate reflection of what happened. My neurologist, Dr. Brightman, said way back in 2006 that it was "so much more than Parkinson's disease." He thought that Shy-Drager or PSP were likely and later landed on Shy-Drager and, more specifically, striatonigral degeneration. Then, in 2012, I had brain surgery, and deep brain stimulators were implanted in my brain to block faulty signals that cause walking and shaking issues.

I have had many benefits from the DBS system that I have implanted in my brain in two areas, and also the generator placed in my chest. This generator is connected to cables that send electrical stimulation to the movement center of my brain. Not many on this earth with atypical parkinsonism have had DBS, so I feel pretty special!

Later, with Dr. Nancy Holcomb, an outstanding movement disorder specialist working with us, I had a DaT scan, which had very notable results that confirmed my atypical parkinsonism syndrome. Afterward, Dr. Nancy Holcomb ordered a PET, which used a radioactive isotope to track metabolism in my brain to determine the type of protein damage there. The proteins in MSA are known as alpha synuclein and develop clumps in brain tissue. The protein found in CBD is called tau, and when it breaks down, it takes the form of tangles. The aggregation of these proteins causes brain degeneration and is incurable and irreversible. Attempts are being made through research to develop methods that will hopefully recognize these degenerative diseases early and possibly arrest them in their progression or even just slow them down. It is probable that cures are a long way off, but we are not out of the fight because we care about future generations who could develop the same type of conditions.

What I have is not genetic and is not communicable. These are syndromes that begin spontaneously or sporadically. It is possibly caused by toxins in the environment, including workplace or dwelling. It's the domino effect of the proteins folding that brings about the loss of neurons that provide for the function of the body: everything from blood pressure regulation, breathing control, swallowing, digestion, urination, eye movements, and gross motor function—to name several but not all of the disabling affects.

I have lost abilities and will continue to decline, but I am still here and loving this life! There is so much going on, and I have so much hope and enthusiasm for my family, faith, and music. I have so much that I want to accomplish each and every day. Though I suffer the effects that these degenerative processes have brought, I have a love for life that is persistent.

My diagnosis has been difficult to understand, let alone explain to others. So many family, friends, contacts, and fellow patients are following my story. As I have explained in my first book, I started writing a blog in 2006 called "PD Plus Me," and though I took the site down for a year or two, I eventually restarted it as "We Will Go On." It is out of that same effort that my pursuit for truth continues.

I want to clarify: it has always been clear since February 2006 that I have an atypical parkinsonian disorder. This much has never been in question, despite the two specialists that caused pain and confusion during the medical leave of my wonderful neurologist, Dr. Brightman. Now, years down the road, the condition has progressed considerably, but my overall strength and heartiness has sustained me. Well, I am still here, right?

When our great neurologist, Dr. Brightman, left our clinic, I was fortunate to be referred by my primary care doctor to a movement disorder specialist in a nearby community. In the process of being diagnosed, I had appointments with Dr. Nancy Holcomb every five to six weeks. She conducted a number of essential tests, as I have stated, including a PET scan, which showed that I had cell degeneration bilaterally in the basal ganglia, the movement center of the brain. I have also had a DaT scan, which indicated degenerative effects in the frontotemporal area on both the left and right sides of my brain.

To date, my diagnosis continues to include corticobasal syndrome and multiple system atrophy. This means that I share movement and balance symptoms that Parkinson's disease patients have, and also so much more. My eye movements grow more and more limited as my ability to move them up and down and side to side becomes gradually more restricted. I also have autonomic dysfunction, which results from a loss of neurons in the areas of the brain that govern the automatic functions of our bodies: urinary, digestion, bowel, swallowing, breathing, blood pressure, body temperature, and heart rate. These are experienced in a much more severe manner than in typical Parkinson's, although no Parkinson's patient escapes these problems—the difference is that it occurs in the first few years of multiple system atrophy and may occur after a decade or more in PD.

I have had changes in medications to determine what side effects might be influential in my symptoms and have also had blood tests to check for genetic mutations or inherited diseases. A scope was put up through my nose and down my throat, resulting in the realization that I have a condition gradually paralyzing my vocal cords, which threatens my ability to breath in the long run. Dr. Nancy Holcomb made us aware of the potential of a tracheostomy procedure to make an airway below my vocal box in order to prevent aspiration pneumonia and also to head off the real possibility of a breathing obstruction emergency.

I am grateful that I have Dr. Nancy Holcomb, a committed, top neurologist who specializes in patients with rare neurodegenerative diseases, along with Parkinson's disease. We are still seeing her and are grateful for her efforts to get a sharper focus on what is bringing about these deadly physical threats to my longevity and have stolen my life from me—career, driving, social life, and freedom to walk around in the world. It isn't that I couldn't accept the reality; it is more that I wanted to have a definitive analysis that now has brought a gift of peace to my soul and spirit.

My dear family would know of what I am referring to and shared my desire for such clarity.

CHAPTER FOUR

Looking Back

After catching up on the latest medical events within the years since I was diagnosed and covering the medical questions and challenges we faced, I am going to circle back for a few pages to discuss some of the places I had been in my life before all of this happened. I was in full swing as a husband and father, with an active family life, church involvement, and a big push to progress in my career. It was in the middle of that fulcrum of Brooks family history that this neurological crisis rudely interrupted.

I discussed some of the general places and faces in the first book, *I Will Go On*, so I want to talk about a few key occurrences that impacted me and set the stage for a big change. In 1990, I applied for, and was selected as, principal at Midland Elementary School in the Moreno Valley School District. I had a successful time there and enjoyed becoming well acquainted with that community. A great PTA, including wonderful parents in general, a really great student body, and some of the best teachers who truly cared about their students. I was very fortunate to be able to work with one of my best friends there, Rick Wallace. Rick taught fourth grade at Midland for many years and was a tremendously talented person. It was fun to be back together on a daily basis, having known each other in high school and college. His father and mother had employed me at the family business called Carwood Carwash. Rick and I met at the carwash and then formed a duo, with him on drums and me on guitar and vocals. Later, I met Michael Healey at Long Beach City College while trying out for the annual homecoming show, and we added Mike (known as Mikael Healey by stage name) as our piano player and additional vocalist. Mike was a tremendously talented player and went on to have a lifelong career in the field of music, with a number of accomplishments, and was truly able to make a living as a great professional musician.

While Rick and I were working together at Midland School, Rick played drums on occasion with me as we joined the students in the all-school talent shows. The students cheered as Mr. Wallace played his drum set and I did my Elvis and Bee Gees impressions. It went over well. Also at Midland were a number of great teachers, all of whom I can't mention, but two stand out as friends for life: Chuck Orr and Larry Keisling. Chuck was instrumental in recommending me as a principal, after starting out as the assistant principal at Midland in 1988. Then I returned to Midland from a stint at Serrano Elementary School as assistant principal, this time as Midland's principal at the age of thirty-four. Chuck was supportive and appreciated the way I handled discipline and worked well with the students, so he told his friend, the superintendent, Mr. Robert C. Lee, that I would make a strong principal. I have always given him credit for planting that seed, and I want to thank him for that. I had to get the master's degree, earn the administrative credential, put in the work in the entry-level jobs, apply, and interview twice for the position (first and second level), but the awareness that Bob Lee had of me and his desire to promote me contributed to my hiring to this position that Chuck had told him I would be able to handle.

Larry was also a wonderful teacher and colleague at Midland. I sang for his fiftieth birthday party and got to know his family. My wife, Karrie, knew his wife through a Bible study fellowship organization where Patty had an administrative roll in the ministry. Karrie was in the program for seven years, studying the entire Bible while helping with the children's ministry for the women who were group leaders and needed their children taught while they were having their weekly preparation meeting. So Larry and I were connected. While we were at Midland together, Larry painted our home as a professional painter. He did a great job and gave us a generously affordable price. Many years later, Larry and I rediscovered our friendship in 2010, meeting at the Riverside Parkinson's Support Group held at the senior center in Riverside. Larry had unfortunately been diagnosed with Parkinson's, and so thirty years later, we were suddenly back in each other's lives, attending meetings and breakfast gatherings with our friends and caregivers with Parkinson's disease in common. Larry recently celebrated his eightieth birthday.

I left Midland, a school that was such a great fit for my life, to take the helm at Butterfield Elementary School in the fall of 1991. I was charged with creating a year-round schedule school that would focus on the arts: music, visual arts, drama, and dance. This school, as described in my first book, was what I consider my greatest achievement in my career. With our success, collectively as a staff, I was recognized as the district's principal of the year and was one of three finalists for county-wide principal of the year. I finished as the runner up, but it was a great experience being chosen for such as honor. Several people stood out at that school, and I had a wonderful staff, with the school secretary, Jerrie Butler, lead clerk, Kathy Benson, and head custodian, Joe Valenzuela, all coming with me from Midland, as did seven teachers who had also taught with me there. Jerrie, Kathy, and Joe worked alongside me for seven years at two sites and became lifelong friends. Jerrie and Kathy have stayed in touch, and we have had intermittent meals and gatherings with them and our other friends from the district, Beth Kleiner,

Terry Witkowski, and Sue Seyfried, over the years. What a blessing to have had so many great friends in the schools.

Jerrie Butler showed me the ropes as a new principal at Midland. She was an excellent school secretary and very dedicated to her responsibilities. She has become a very close friend in the thirty-three years we have known her. She has remained in touch with Karrie and me and has had us over to her home a number of times. We love her and feel her love and care as well.

Joe Valenzuela supported me like a brother. He was a wonderfully dedicated head custodian and believed in our vision for a school that provided artistic instruction along with strong academics to round out a child's education. He succumbed to esophageal cancer a couple of years ago after we were able to get together two or three times to play guitars and have a coffee together. I regret not having had more time to spend with him over the years after I moved on from Butterfield.

I encountered a variety of challenges and dealt with negative people through those years. I had challenges from parents, some justified and some not, but they tended to take their toll. One such time a parent challenged our school plan and wanted to rewrite it. It was inappropriate for the district administration to allow a parent to singlehandedly force the school principal to change a plan written by staff and approved by the school site council. Nevertheless, the administrator I reported to at the time held an all-day session, during which she, the district level leader, the parent site council member, and I shared a district-provided lunch and edited the school plan that had been duly written and approved by our school site council. It irked me to go through this process. Though I never minded input and critique, I felt that this supervisor had dishonored me and did not uphold the district procedure for such practices. It was somewhat humiliating and taught me to be a bit more circumspect about trusting those I would serve under in the future.

I toughened up more and more as I reached age forty and was an independent principal who followed district direction but took the leadership of my school sites from that point on with more autonomy in mind. I realized that taking care of my teachers and students, while consulting with our parents, was my priority, and political games were not to take precedence over our local school priorities and community culture.

Another negative experience that has to be mentioned was the destructive behavior of one of my employees who was in the custodial department. He was a fellow who worked at night and was a person with several challenges that affected his work and attendance. He was apparently using illicit substances and acted out behaviorally with episodes of anger. He also struggled financially and had trouble being at work regularly—but more so, being on time. I worked with him to take care of these issues, and when it didn't work out, I had to let him go. The next day I was alone in my office, after the students and most of the teachers and staff had left for the evening. It was around 5:30 p.m., and it was the late fall, so it was dark outside as I sat at my desk. I would normally have been there until around 6:00 p.m., but I had finished up and left for the day. Typically, when the crew was coming around to clean the office, we would leave some lights on so that my office was lit up. When I returned in the morning, a large commercial-sized hexagonal brick was laying on the floor across the room from the window, fifteen feet away. The wall had a crushed area where the brick had obviously struck it. There in its wake was a broken window, shattered by the assailant, who had picked up and tossed the brick hard enough go through the window and hit the wall at the opposite side of the room!

The path that it traveled through the air, in my mind's eye, passed right through the side table where I normally typed each evening as I did my computer work and wrote my reports for teacher reviews and evaluations, among other documents and tasks. If I had stayed, the brick would have struck me. I was close to that window, while the wall, which it hit hard enough to leave a significant dent, was another ten feet past it. A crazy thing to imagine, but the man whom I had fired the day before was a big guy with the potential strength to do just the deed that I am describing. Whew! This kind of occurrence wasn't daily, but there are a number of stories like this that I could tell and won't add to the book. The important thing was the work that we were doing for kids, and the risks, though not something to overlook, were part of the price of being in charge of a large organization that made a difference in the lives of students, parents, teachers, and staff. Stress like this, though, when you are destined to have a brain disease, is very possibly a contributing factor in triggering the initiation of a degenerative condition such as mine.

I was principal at Butterfield for five years, and our success there earned me a promotion to Landmark Middle School, where I had two full-time assistant principals to help lead a magnet program in math, science, and technology that was already in place. This would be my second principalship at a magnet school, and it had a population of over 1500 students. I earned the district-wide principal of the year award from the PTA council in the spring of 1997 before moving on to the Alvord Unified School District. Landmark went well, though I did miss my first love, the elementary school principalship, and I left to get that role back the following year. I left there, going on to Promenade School.

Promenade was a year-round school, with a kinder-garten-through-sixth grade population. While there I led the conversion from a three-track to four-track calendar, guided them successfully through an English Language Learner program California State review, and led them through a reconstruction project, which saw every building in the school refurbished. While there for four years, I started my doctoral studies that led to the completion of my educational doctorate degree in 2003.

One occurrence stood out as most challenging. While I was standing out in front of the school, waiting for the final bell to supervise the students being picked up, a man drove up in the circle, threatening to shoot me. I stayed out there, thinking that I couldn't endanger my students or staff, so I was willing to do my job if that meant being the target. The bell rang, and he eventually left, but I reported the situation to the police and the school district administration. An arrest was made, and he was charged with making a terrorist threat on a public official and was put in custody for a few weeks, only to be seen back on the street within a few weeks of this horrible occurrence. These and many other situations over the years took their toll, but the positives in my career far outweighed these and many other difficult situations that I don't have time to describe. I sought counseling to deal with the posttraumatic stress that these situations brought.

One day earlier in my years at Promenade, I saw three dogs attacking students across the street. I stopped four lanes of traffic, walked across the street, and yelled at those three large dogs. One, an Akita, had a nine-year-old boy by the meat of his thigh and was shaking him with his teeth, clutching the largest part of the child's leg. I yelled at the dog to let go, lunging toward him, and he released his grip and dropped the student. I cradled him in my arms and rushed across the street to the school office to get an ambulance to come attend to him. The boy survived but was greatly impacted by this event.

At Promenade, I was blessed to hire and befriend David Collier. I interviewed and hired him in 1998, and we found that we had a number of interests in common, including our Christian faith and the love of books. The second year we worked together, David's ailing heart became weaker as time went along, to the point that he was in desperate need of a transplant. He came close to death and was successful in finding a donor to provide a young, healthy heart that could replace his own that was failing him. His heart rebirth is June 20, the same as the day of the year I was born in 1955. David recovered and has done well. He recently reached his twentieth year with his new heart, and there has been no sign of rejection! We attended a men's two-day revival event during those years together. He and I continue to be friends to this day, having met regularly for breakfast one Saturday each month for about fifteen years. This has, unfortunately, been interrupted by my tracheostomy because I can no longer eat (Let's not even mention the pandemic that broke out, closing down inside dining for most of a year or better). I appreciate David's support and prayers over the many years we have been friends.

Moving to Terrace School in 2001, after four years at Promenade, I had a great time getting to know Doug

Allen, Lance Paddock, and Mark Richici. They became my friends to this day and have been there to support me as I have gone through the wiles of atypical parkinsonism these last fifteen years. Also at Terrace, I was able to bring over a great secretary named Pat Miller, who I spent four years with at Promenade then another couple of years at Terrace. She stayed on there after I left, until her retirement. Pat was a true friend whom I could put my trust in, and she ran a very organized, smooth desk. She handled many important details and was one to prayerfully support me as a leader. Pat is someone I will always be grateful for as a colleague and friend. Again, I can't name everyone, but I will say that Terrace had one of the most professional, dedicated staffs that I have ever had the pleasure to know and lead.

After finishing my doctorate, I went on to become the director and then assistant superintendent of human resources for Beaumont Unified School District, and I served in that role from 2003 to 2007, when I was forced to retire due to the rise of the brain disease that I developed. The story of working at Beaumont during this time of change is well enough covered in my first book.

I started out as a teacher aide in 1976 at Starr King Elementary School in Long Beach Unified School District and taught five years at Bret Harte School, before serving as a Program Facilitator in charge of projects. I served in that role for part of a year at Harte, as well as another school year at Clara Barton Elementary School, from 1986 to 1987. It was then that Karrie and I decided to move with our two sons, Daniel and Mark, and one son on the way, Stephen, to Moreno Valley. We started our lives as homeowners and grew with our family as we enjoyed a close-knit community of schools, sports teams, scouting, and churches. We enjoyed our lives there tremendously between 1987 and 1996, when we moved to Riverside. I deeply appreciated those thirty-one years working in the public schools and had no desire to stop when I did. I had plans to move on to the superintendency in the following years, as I began to feel the effects of a degenerative brain condition that was insidiously stealing my health and my career from me.

My family, Karrie, Daniel and Jenny, Mark and Sarah, Stephen and Kelley, along with our five—going on six—grandchildren, have paid a great price for all that has happened to me medically. They say that the patient doesn't have the disease alone, that the close family members also bear the scars of the fatal illness, too, and go through it with you. I have been saddened about how much our young adult children, in those early years of diagnosis, had to grow up as they were finishing college, establishing their careers, getting married, and having children, all while trying their best to support Karrie and me as we went through the many changes that came. Every time I've been hospitalized, had surgery, or received a more serious diagnosis, they have been there for me. I am so grateful for the joy of our grandchildren: Naomi, Mariamne, William, Jack, Enid, and *a baby to be named later*, who have inspired me and made me the happiest man in the world. Thank you for making Karrie and me grandparents! That is the greatest honor anyone could bestow on another person.

CHAPTER FIVE

Atypical Parkinsonism: Insidious and Elusive

Introduction

I would like to step back for a chapter to take the time to review and explain the atypical parkinsonian syndromes. Atypical parkinsonism syndromes conditions involve the degeneration of the basal ganglia, the movement center of the brain. Parkinson's disease and Parkinson's plus will generally affect this part of the brain in that both will have a loss of the cells that produce a chemical called dopamine. Dopamine is required by the brain in order to bring about normal and properly coordinated movements. This lack of dopamine causes the symptoms of Parkinson's disease that are sometimes found in atypical parkinsonism, such as tremors, postural instability (balance difficulty), rigidity (stiffness), and bradykinesia (slowness of movement).

Although the atypical parkinsonism syndromes generally have some aspects of these symptoms resulting from dopamine loss, atypical parkinsonism is not merely another name for Parkinson's disease or a more serious version, but it is a disease which includes Parkinson's disease symptoms, plus other serious conditions.

As brain cells are lost or damaged, the symptoms will also worsen and affect speech, swallowing, balance, walking, tremors, eye movements, bodily functions, stiffness, and facial expression, to name a few of the issues that are more prevalent. Cognition (the thinking process) is affected and is one of the least noticed but most severe aspects of atypical parkinsonism.

Differences Between Parkinson's Plus and Idiopathic Parkinson's Disease

Patients with atypical parkinsonism syndromes have a worse prognosis than those with Parkinson's disease (PD), and atypical parkinsonism syndromes respond poorly to the standard anti-Parkinson's disease treatments. Although the medications used may be similar to those used to treat Parkinson's disease, atypical parkinsonism syndromes typically do not respond as well to these medications. An inadequate response to treatment in a patient with Parkinson's disease–like symptoms may indicate that an atypical parkinsonism syndrome is developing. This should trigger medical tests and a thorough examination in search of any signs of degeneration in other brain structures beyond the basal ganglia.

Parkinsonism-plus syndromes typically progress more rapidly than Parkinson's disease. There is no cure for these conditions, so treatment focuses on managing symptoms.

Diagnosing Parkinson's Plus

It is often difficult to diagnose an atypical parkinsonism condition to the point of determining which of the particular syndromes it is, specifically. Like Parkinson's disease, identifying specific biomarkers is difficult, and the diagnosis of these diseases is primarily a clinical process of observation. In some cases, the diagnosis is confirmed after death when the brain is then studied and it becomes possible to differentiate. The parts of the brain affected with cell loss or shrinkage will determine which of the symptoms are manifested; thus, the diagnosis is based on the symptoms that are emphasized in each condition.

The term "carbidopa/levodopa" refers to the most important and common medication used to treat hallmark symptoms, and it is usually most effective in cases of regular Parkinson's disease. Carbidopa/levopoda is only moderately helpful in the case of atypical parkinsonism. This distinction about the effectiveness of carbidopa/levodopa is one of the most important differences between regular (idiopathic) Parkinson's when compared to atypical parkinsonism.

Multiple System Atrophy

Multiple system atrophy (MSA) is a rare degenerative condition and has historically been called Shy-Drager syndrome as well. In MSA, more widespread neurological damage occurs than in the case of Parkinson's. Both Parkinson's disease and multiple system atrophy produce a buildup of alpha synuclein proteins in brain cells of the basal ganglia where dopamine is produced. In multiple system atrophy, the damage to cells is more widespread within the brain. When compared with Parkinson's disease, multiple system atrophy affects more areas that control important autonomic functions, such as heart rate, breathing, blood pressure, urination, digestion, body temperature, eye movements, and sweating. Multiple system atrophy does not respond as well to anti-Parkinson's disease medicines, if it responds at all. Conversely, Parkinson's disease responds well to these medications, which helps doctors to make that diagnosis. Multiple system atrophy progresses more quickly than Parkinson's. Multiple system atrophy has an average survival rate of seven to ten years, though in some cases patients have been known to live as long as fifteen years or more, while Parkinson's disease does not necessarily affect the longevity of the patient. These are key differences between these two diseases, but by no means all of them.

The two different MSA subtypes are identified based on which areas of the brain are most affected. MSA may appear to be a typical case of PD in the first few years of disease onset, but as it progresses, extreme drops in blood pressure upon rising from a chair (accompanied by dizziness), difficulty with bowel and bladder control, exaggerated pulse rate fluctuations, and sexual impotence will give rise to this diagnosis. Milly Kondracke, whose life was presented in a book and made-for-TV movie called *Saving Milly*, was diagnosed with Parkinson's disease initially, but she was believed to have had a case of MSA when she died. There are two subtypes of MSA, as described below.

Multiple System Atrophy-Parkinsonism (MSA-P)

This subtype is difficult in the initial years to distinguish from Parkinson's disease. Tremors, balance issues, rigidity, speech, and swallowing are all eventually affected. It will be distinguished from idiopathic PD by its faster onset and inadequate response to carbidopa/levodopa therapy. The autonomic issues will also become progressively worse as the disease progresses.

Multiple System Atrophy-Cerebellar (MSA-C)

This one is also similar to PD, but because of damage to the area of the brain called the cerebellum, balance, walking gait issues, eye movement abnormalities, and speech are affected more severely. The walking gait difficulty that surfaces with MSA-C is called ataxia. Challenges with the overall coordination of bodily movements is the striking difference between this and the other subtype. The prominent features are an unsteady, staggering walk with slurred speech. Autonomic system functions will eventually be harmed as well.

Progressive Supranuclear Palsy

Progressive supranuclear palsy (PSP) often resembles Parkinson's disease. Changes in the protein tau lead to neural degeneration. These changes lead to an aggregation of fibrillar polymers, known as taupathies. Its unique features include early development of a severe loss of balance, unsteady walking, and frequent falls. People with PSP also may develop blurred vision and impaired eyesight, especially the inability to look up or down. This lack of eye movement causes difficulty for the patient to see where he or she is going and interferes with reading and eating. Other symptoms include a gradual but significant impairment in speech and swallowing. Apathy, depression, and a reduced ability to think are common among patients with PSP.

No medication has been found to treat this disorder. As with the other atypical parkinsonism conditions, PD drugs such as carbidopa/levodopa and dopamine agonists are sometimes mildly beneficial and worth attempting as treatments. Currently, medical interventions are aimed at reducing the impact of specific symptoms, such as balance, eating, and swallowing. Support, counseling, and education for patients and care partners can improve the patient's quality of life. The average survival from onset of symptoms is seven years.

Corticobasal Ganglionic Degeneration

CBD is a movement disorder that usually starts after age sixty. Like progressive supranuclear palsy, it is a taupathy (see above in first paragraph of PSP explanation). First, symptoms often appear on one side of the body and spread to the other side. They include stiffness, rigidity, slowness, tremor, jerky movements, and loss of sensation. Later, patients can develop problems with walking and maintaining balance, dementia, memory loss, and "alien limb" phenomenon, a condition in which a limb appears to move on its own. Depression and other emotional changes may also develop.

Carbidopa/levodopa treatment is rarely successful. Other medicines may help manage specific symptoms. Physical, occupational, and speech therapy can help patients cope with the illness. Education and support can improve quality of life. The average survival from the onset of symptoms is eight years.

Lewy Body Disease

Lewy bodies are abnormal protein deposits found in brain cells. In Parkinson's disease, Lewy bodies form in only one area of the brain, the basal ganglia (where dopamine cells are lost, reducing the dopamine needed for normal movement). In Lewy body disease (LBD), these deposits are found in other important areas of the brain, as well.

Symptoms of LBD are similar to Parkinson's and Alzheimer's diseases, with an overwhelming emphasis on dementia characteristics. In addition, patients can have repeated visual hallucinations and experience varying levels of alertness and mental ability. Depression, apathy, anxiety, and delusional thoughts also are common. Some patients develop a sleep disorder years before developing LBD that may cause them to violently and loudly act out their dreams.

Treatment with levodopa and some Alzheimer's medications are sometimes helpful. Support, education, and counseling for the patient and family are important. The average survival from onset of symptoms is five to seven years. LBD has many overlapping symptoms with MSA, and the two can be confused in the diagnostic process until later progression or a brain autopsy can determine the pathology that developed prior to death.

I have corticobasal syndrome—or CBS. Formerly, this would have been named corticobasal ganglionic degeneration or CBGD. Today, corticobasal syndrome is the handle given to this illness during the life of the patient because it has to be confirmed pathologically with an autopsy of the brain tissue after the passing of the patient. All atypical parkinsonism syndromes, multiple system atrophy, progressive supranuclear palsy, Lewy body dementia, and corticobasal degeneration are not diagnosed absolutely until a brain study can be completed. The diagnosis is called "probable" or "possible" during the life of the patient.

So, after fifteen years of treatment for atypical parkinsonism—thought to be multiple system atrophy (MSA)—it has been determined that I do have MSA and also corticobasal syndrome. The reasons are that I have the movement disorder and cognitive symptoms of CBS, but I also have the neurologically caused autonomic failure of MSA. I have explained this dysautonomia condition earlier in the book, and you may want to refer back to it, or you may read more about it my book, *I Will Go On: Living with a Movement Disorder* (BookSurge, 2009). In this chapter, I will now explain the basics of coriticobasal syndrome in greater detail.

Overview of Corticobasal Syndrome

Corticobasal syndrome is a movement disorder that is similar to Parkinson's disease, though it is faster progressing and includes additional symptomatic issues that are more complicated earlier in the disease process than in Parkinson's disease. Parkinson's disease is similar because it has symptoms known as parkinsonism, which include 1) tremor, 2) balance problems, 3) stiffness, and 4) slowness—all caused by a degeneration of brain neurons. Because coriticobasal syndrome also involves the basal ganglia (the movement control center of the brain that is also involved in Parkinson's), some of the symptoms overlap; thus, it is an atypical parkinsonism syndrome.

That is where the similarity stops. I do not have Parkinson's, and I never have. From the beginning, my neurologist at the time said, "This is so much more than Parkinson's disease."

It was thought to be either progressive supranuclear palsy or Shy-Drager (an earlier name given to the condition now referred to as multiple system atrophy). Progressive supranuclear palsy is a close cousin to coricobasal syndrome, so we have been in the right arena over the past fifteen years. The treatment and care given to me were helpful and would have been the same with either designation. I still would have had the brain surgery that I had in July 2012, and it would have been considered helpful and effective in giving me better movement and more ability to walk with assistance, rather than being in a wheelchair most of the time, as I had been prior to the deep brain stimulation surgery.

What is Corticobasal Syndrome?

Corticobasal syndrome is a movement disorder that includes walking trouble, tremors/jerky movements, eye control movement impairment, swallowing difficulty, rigidity, and balance trouble. It also causes cognitive changes that affect behavior, speech, mood problems, and difficulty planning and concentrating. It is a form of dementia called frontotemporal dementia, but it is not the same disease as other forms of dementia, such as Alzheimer's disease (AD). It should not be confused with AD, although it can be in its presentation.

What Causes Corticobasal Syndrome?

It is not clear what causes the degenerative process in the brain of individuals with CBS, but what we do know is that there is a specific protein in the brain known as tau that breaks down and creates tangles. These tangles destroy nerve pathways and inhibit the ability of the brain to communicate signals that help us move—whether through coordinating movements, walking, talking, grasping, swallowing, or seeing.

What is Alien Limb Syndrome?

One of the symptoms of CBS is a phenomenon called alien limb syndrome, in which a hand, arm, or leg seems to have a mind of its own, assuming postures and movements that are alien to the patient's awareness. Also, there are twisted postures of hands, fingers, arms, neck, legs, and feet. These movements may also manifest in a jerky, unpredictable manner; while a form of tremor in some, it may be less regular and random in its form. Parkinson's disease typically, when tremor exists (not all Parkinson's patients have tremors), has a slow, regularly patterned tremor that occurs generally during rest.

What is a Taupathy?

The illnesses that are caused by the breakdown of the protein tau include Alzheimer's disease and progressive supranuclear palsy, along with corticobasal syndrome.

How is it treated?

CBS does not have a cure, but there are a number of treatments that may help with symptom relief. Some of the medicines used for Parkinson's are also given to those with CBS, which has been true in my case. Sinemet, also known as carbidopa/levadopa, is given to help some with rigidity and tremor. I do receive some benefit from Sinemet. Other treatments address the cognitive issues and can include medicines used to assist with memory. Speech therapy can be used to assist with swallowing problems, which has been beneficial in my case. Swallowing problems have to be combated because they can lead to serious choking and eventual pneumonia. Falling and gait difficulty require physical therapy and assistive devices such as canes, walkers, wheelchairs, and electric scooters. I use all of the above. Special lenses may be prescribed to help with the eye movement control problems. These would be meant to help to prevent double vision. This eye-aiming and movement problem occurs in both progressive supranuclear palsy and corticobasal syndrome. These two syndromes are often confused with one another, and a brain study post-mortem is the only way to distinguish which is the correct diagnosis. Both will show tau tangles in the brain tissue.

In Summary

Understand that my explanation is from my personal reading and is by no means a scientific description. Rather, think of it as a start toward me helping you, the reader, gain knowledge about that with which I am struggling. I see the writing of this book as an opportunity to clarify the process by which I am continuing my effort toward positive forward motion in life. This is a daily decision and a better choice than sitting down and giving up. Along with CBS, I am fighting the low body temperature regulation problems, the falling blood pressure (orthostatic hypotension), trouble with urination, digestive dysfunction, breathing difficulty, and heartbeat irregularities—all of which are caused by a breaking down of neurons from a different cause than CBS. MSA involves the misfolding of alpha synuclein protein, rather than tau tangles. It is being found that some patients have *both proteins* causing neurodegeneration. Diseases aren't fair and don't "leave you alone" because you already struggle with another condition. There is no rule that you can't get two neurodegenerative diseases. The following web address provides an article that gives an example of how these two proteins and their misfolding can work together in the disease process (see: https://mayoclinic.pure.elsevier.

com/en/publications/alpha-synuclein-and-tau-team-mates-in-neurodegeneration).

Hopefully, this specificity will help to explain the differences that make my condition an exception to the more common brain illness known as Parkinson's disease. Henceforth, I will hope to be part of the effort to bring light to this serious condition known as corticobasal syndrome. I am very thankful for the exceptional movement disorder specialist I am treated by who investigated my brain disease very thoroughly and with all relevant technology and advanced diagnostic techniques. I have so much to be thankful for, including my caregiving spouse, Karrie, who loves me and shows such grace and patience in dealing with all of the inabilities and changes that affect her nearly as much as me. Also, I thank my sons, their spouses, and our grandchildren, who are with me frequently and are helpful and encouraging to me in making the most of every day.

CHAPTER SIX

Living on with Disease Progression

Adjusting to Decline with Family Support

With both multiple system atrophy and corticobasal syndrome symptoms occurring simultaneously, I am learning to adjust to the changes. I find a need for scooting around in my transport wheelchair more these days. I just take the footrests off of the chair, and I can move around the house pretty well. The great thing about the smaller transfer chair is that it does not have the large wheels, so it is narrower and fits through hallways and doorways as I enter the restroom and bedrooms. I can spend hours in this transport chair and it is quite comfortable.

I am having a difficult time accepting that I have the cognitive behavioral dysfunctions that accompany CBS/FTD. Corticobasal syndrome is a part of the broader neurodegenerative disease known as frontotemporal degeneration. I take Namenda to slow the progression of dementia that is associated with CBS.

Karrie is so helpful and understanding. We are focusing on family and friends. We appreciate the support of our adult kids, their wonderful spouses, and their beautiful children. It is a tight group!

The local Parkinson's support group is a great place to share with patients and caregivers. Online, we stay in touch through CurePSP "go to meeting" groups. And, of course, our church is a great support and a caring family. We also are active members in the Multiple System Atrophy Coalition support group and have been for many years.

Where Does the MSA, PSP, or CBD Patient Fit?

I have been an outlier for years. It is the nature of the beast. I have an atypical parkinsonian disorder, namely corticobasal syndrome with multiple system atrophy. These syndromes are so similar to each other that they can be paired in my brain and are hard to tell apart in another case where it would be considered one or the other. I have defined and summarized these syndromes, so I will not consider those questions further.

The issue I want to broach is support. Support groups are a major factor in seeking support and education. In these settings trust is established and fostered by the leaders and group members at large.

Let's take a few minutes and step back to look at my diagnostic history. Those who have read my first book *We Will Go On* are aware that Dr. Brightman was my original neurologist who diagnosed me with an atypical parkinsonism disorder. He conducted tests and examined me, concluding that what I had was "so much more than Parkinson's disease." That was in February 2006. He said progressive supranuclear palsy and Shy-Drager were the likely diagnoses. Over the years he sharpened the focus somewhat, but eventually he decided my case was unique enough that atypical parkinsonism was the most closely defined that he could confidently label my case.

As stated earlier, in 2012, Dr. Brightman referred me to Dr. Merrill Morgan, who conducted deep brain stimulation surgery in order to place two implants in my brain and one in my chest. This treatment, though risky and hard to undergo, was a success in that it has increased my overall health, lengthening my life. This surgery was not a cure and is still benefiting me, though less and less over time.

Previously, I explained that four years ago I was fortunate to be referred to neurology at a respected clinic near our home, and I was paired with a movement disorder specialist. She ran tests, including DaT and PET scans, and she videotaped my condition as I walked and moved my limbs and eyes. She spent a great deal of time with us, and we also met with a team of doctors, who entered the exam room and contributed their opinions.

Dr. Nancy Holcomb determined that what I have is corticobasal syndrome with multiple system atrophy. I have a very long list of symptoms, which, again, are well covered in this and my first book as well. Among those symptoms are several movement issues that fall under the description of parkinsonism. Parkinsonism describes symptoms that are found in Parkinson's disease—walking trouble, shaking, balance problems, and slow movements. Because I have parkinsonism, along with autonomic disorders, frontotemporal issues, neurologically based eye-aiming struggles, and swallowing issues that can cause pneumonia, I have always tended to gather with Parkinson's disease patients. Parkinson's disease affects one percent of the population over sixty years old. Atypical parkinsonian syndromes are rare and only represent approximately three percent of the total Parkinson's disease population. The size of the group that is represented by PD means that there are support groups available in much greater prevalence.

As reported in an earlier chapter, Karrie and I were attending a Parkinson's disease support group in a nearby coastal region as early as January 2006. We enjoyed that group for two years and were recruited by the Riverside Parkinson's Support Group in November 2006. We joined that group, stating from the beginning that I had a different disorder that shared some of the same symptoms. We have developed many friendships in the RPSG over these fifteen-plus years, and Karrie and I led the group for most of four years between 2007 and 2011. After all that time, it became clear that my atypical parkinsonian disorder was not relevant enough to the needs of the patients, caregivers, and leaders that were found in that group. We loved and cared for these folks and their leaders but decided it would be best that we not attend the sessions, knowing that my diseases—which have some overlap with Parkinson's but are arguably faster progressing and more life threatening in the immediate sense—were frightening to the general group.

This support group issue is not peculiar to me; it is a universal problem that needs to be addressed by the movement disorder and neurodegenerative brain disease community. I had been fortunate to be welcomed and cared for by the original coastal group that we initially joined, and we are grateful for all the years that we attended and supported the Riverside group. We have been involved in online groups concurrently, such as CurePSP, MSA Coalition, Brain Support Network, and a number of other organizations. With these, we have had the chance to participate in online chats, but face-to-face meetings are a rare thing we have experienced only three or four times. There was a movement by CurePSP that Vera James and Lorreta Mazorra provided leadership for as groups were gathered in Los Angeles at UCLA and at a coastal university located an hour from our home. Robin Riddle of the Brain

Support Network has organized an atypical parkinsonian syndrome support group in the San Francisco Bay area, and she has made a number of us outside of that region honorary members.

I couldn't be more thankful to have had the opportunity to know so many of the people in these groups, and so many have unselfishly listened, provided resources, and taken time to voluntarily support families like ours, with a rare disease that overlaps somewhat with Parkinson's.

The point is that those of us with corticobasal syndrome, multiple system atrophy, progressive supranuclear palsy, and Lewy body dementia are not frequently able to find a group in which we fit. Typically, it is helpful if the Parkinson's disease support groups are able to recognize the reality that a small but important percentage of the PD support group participants will eventually be diagnosed with an atypical parkinsonian disorder. It is because of this fact that years ago I would lead discussions at the Riverside PSG in order to inform the patients, caregivers, and their families about the signs of such a diagnosis so that they would be able to recognize the onset of such a syndrome.

I am an outlier as a patient who does not specifically have Parkinson's disease. There are people throughout the United States and across the world who have this same distinction. All of us could need support groups, if we choose to avail ourselves of them. I am advocating for more atypical parkinsonian groups to be formed within a reasonable driving distance so that patients and caregivers are able to support one another and learn from one another's experiences. When this can't be accomplished, Parkinson's disease groups need to be better informed about the facts concerning MSA, CBS, PSP, and LBD and open their doors to these conditions. All atypical parkinsonian patients will benefit, as will Parkinson's disease patients and their families.

Adapting to Changes

For a short while, our local clinic had a neurologist whose specialty was movement disorders like atypical parkinsonism syndromes. We temporarily returned to the local clinic for the opportunity to see this wonderful doctor without needing referrals and approvals. She agreed with my previous movement disorder specialist that what I have are two atypical parkinsonism syndromes. After two visits, she asked that we return to the clinic where Dr. Nancy Holcomb was a movement disorder specialist. She was taking an extended family leave. Good for her.

So as I return to continue writing after a hiatus lasting months, I am revealing what has been happening and why Karrie and I have been overwhelmed. I am self-conscious about the nature of my diagnosis and what it means. In the meantime, I am not sure how this fits with an existence that is more and more limited. I choose to live each day to its fullest, no matter how limited I am. Adapting to the changing of specialists over the years isn't for the faint hearted, but it is doable.

I Couldn't Stop Shaking

I couldn't stop shaking. The night was creeping in, and I tried to sleep but couldn't. Then it dawned on me. *I am overwhelmed.* Thanks to a recent visit from a dear family member, I was made aware that it is okay to realize this—that I was in a tough spot. I don't have to keep a stiff upper lip and try to convince myself that all is fine, when sometimes it is not.

It is enough sometimes just to keep it all straight. I am not always able to do so, but I give it my best. I think being ill with a neurological disease of this magnitude is all encompassing, and I am trying to make sense of something that is not very definable. And let me say, though I may seem to be out of touch and unaware of the great love and grace of our heavenly Father, I am not actually. I just have a hard time putting it all in context sometimes. It is as though I am trying to sort out the reality of this life as a man impaired, and then, at the same time, I want to be able to go on in the strength of all I once held. It isn't an easy task on any day, for any human being, let alone one who is brain impaired.

You see, "You look the same," as I often hear it, isn't enough for me. We with Parkinson's and Parkinson's-like diseases don't always look impaired or so different from our previous status that we held prior to the changes these diseases brought forth. We are simply working at keeping it all together. We shake, yes, and sometimes the shaking can be overwhelming and very challenging. But it involves much more than shaking.

I was outside in our yard with my daughter-in-law's father, Steve Thornton, who had come to visit, and the trembling became just so unreasonably strong that, for a moment, I could barely think of the conversation. It was such a nice visit and so fulfilling a discussion that I was able to set aside the constant trembling inside my whole body and the continual nodding of my head well enough to respond and learn from a wonderful and caring person. I learned so much from that talk because there was a great perception of my station, an empathy that touched a place deep within, and I was strengthened as a result. My point: there is much more going on than the very obvious "shaking." The other medical challenges persist, too. This all comes with the package. The health struggles are enough, but capping it all off is a mind that is affected greatly. My personality is on overload, and I try to keep the rudder of my ship steering the real me on the right course, but it isn't so easy to do. I will always be grateful to Steve for being there to talk and listen to that day.

Tonight I awoke troubled, and it dawned on me. When I can't stop shaking, it isn't just my body but my whole being. Who I am now, who I was before. Yes, this disease is part of me now, as my caring visitor reminded me. There is no turning back. But if I seem less able to put it all together than I once could, don't think I am being unreasonable or less faithful to my beliefs. Sometimes the questions are more real than the answers. But I am not throwing in the towel; on the contrary, I am opening the door to places that most of us have never walked or experienced. It is lonely through that door, and I don't exactly understand or know where it is leading me. I am trying, but sometimes I just can't stop shaking.

These Days I Sit On Corner Stones

"These days I sit on corner stones and count the time in quarter tones to ten, my friend, Don't confront me with my failures, I had not forgotten them." Those are two of my favorite lines to a song that I like to play and sing by Jackson Browne called "These Days." These phrases relate to my existence with multiple system atrophy in that they describe a man of introspection. In this specific case, a review of the past and how today does or doesn't fit the person I was at that time. I sit on a cornerstone more often to think, like the big boulders we had in our last yard that were not the most comfortable place to perch but were a setting that invited a sit-and-think session.

But figuratively, I sit at home as a non-driver, within my daily pleasant but confined contemplation. This confinement is not all bad. To the contrary, it is a freedom that I did not have when I was running the race of a career that I loved and poured myself into—that of managing and leading educational institutions. My focus was kids. Now, I proudly focus on my three grown kids and their loved ones. I am particularly aware of our grandchildren, who are so special to us. Naomi was our first in 2012, and she brought a renewed sense of purpose and motivation to our lives in a way that no one else could in the circumstances at that time. I had just had deep brain stimulation surgery a few months prior to her arrival. She is eight now, and I don't believe she sees multiple system atrophy when she sees me; she sees what I still think must be a dream Grandpa—wow, that is me!

These thoughts lead to an awareness that my body is hard to control as I skid my loafers around on the ceramic tile floor and work at maintaining my vertical status. I think about rising from a chair to do a simple task and waiting fifteen seconds before launching myself on the trip to the kitchen to get a drink of water. "Don't begin to walk until you make sure you have blood pressure in your head," I tell myself. I have recorded blood pressure as low as seventy over fifty at a physician's appointment. I am still evaluated by the outside world as to what degree my jerking and tremors have increased or decreased, which will always fluctuate depending on the DBS settings and when I last had my appointment to adjust them. Or the degree to which my medicines are working or wearing off, which is after two-and-a-half hours in the case of carbodopa-levodopa. Now, my autonomic difficulty has progressed beyond it being manageable. These issues include breathing, swallowing, aiming my eyes, and "voiding" becoming more and more difficult, if not nearly impossible, to manage.

No, I don't live in fear. I live in hope. Hope that I will continue to view the world as a beautiful place to explore, even if at times I must do so from an armchair. Days are precious. Breathing, eating, laughing, seeing, hearing, standing, and playing my instruments fill my days. These are reasons to be alive. I am—in this state, with all that MSA has brought to my brain and body—enough.

"These days I seem to think a lot, about the things that I forgot to do, for you. And all the times I had the chance to…" ("These Days" by Jackson Browne). What matters most are the lives we affect that are closest to us. These days are good days because you—*you*, I say—are what I want to fill "These Days" with…enough.

Jackson Browne is a family favorite, stemming from the fact that Karrie and I both loved his music before we met forty years ago and found it to be a commonality that added to the power of our bond. Walking by our front door, you may hear one of his CDs playing to this day.

Off the Cliff of Emotion

It was a typical Sunday morning at church. I was playing on stage with the worship team, for which I played guitar and sang vocals. I lost something that morning that I had held on to throughout my life, even after atypical parkinsonism entered the picture. In spite of everything this neurological disease had caused, I had been able to sing and play on stage. It was hard, after my diagnosis, to get up and down on the platform at church, and I am not saying that there had been no effect on my musical abilities, since I had been diagnosed at that point for seven years. However, I was somehow always able to sing my song and play my own accompaniment, without failing to complete a song in performance. As a songwriter who performed concerts in my late teens and into my mid-twenties, as a musician and singer who played in worship bands in churches off and on my entire life up to the writing of this book, I did it well. As a wedding singer who performed as a minstrel, often performing four to five songs during church wedding ceremonies as a side profession for many years and as an entertainer playing for banquets, schools and churches until my tracheotomy operation in January 2020, I have never failed to finish a song. On this particular Sunday in 2013, it happened. It was defeating.

I was singing the song "Give Me Jesus," a traditional song recorded by Fernando Ortega that I was singing and finger picking in a folk style. A portion of the lyrics read the following:

Verse 1:
In the morning, when I rise
In the morning, when I rise

In the morning, when I rise
Give me Jesus.
Chorus:
Give me Jesus, Give me Jesus
You can have all of this world
But give me Jesus.

I had sung this, and the second verse followed by the chorus, and everything had gone well. Then, as a neurological patient, I came to the third verse, which triggered a weeping spell. This brought my collapse.

I began the third verse, singing, "When I come to die…" and as I went to repeat those words two more times, I opened my mouth and squeaked out, "When I come to die…" and at that moment, I could barely say the word "die." My family was sitting in the second row, and I realized the cruelty of those words. Having a disease which had an average life expectancy of seven to fifteen years made these words, sung as my family listened, seem sad and cruel. I began to weep, and the more I wept, the less I was able to open my mouth and sing the words. I played the guitar and never stopped playing the accompaniment. I tried to mouth the words further, and after a couple of lines, the choir leader named John, who was behind me, began to softly sing for me, and others joined in. Soon many were singing the words as I wept and sobbed, continuing to finger pick my Guild guitar.

At the conclusion of my playing and crying, my wife and caregiver, Karrie, instinctively knew she needed to come up on the platform and guide me down. I don't walk well, having coordination and balance problems that interfere with my ability to walk. But more than that, I was an emotional mess, and I needed her comfort. We hugged in front of a full church, which holds about 200. Others were shedding tears. My son, Mark, who plays the drums in our band at church, reached out and comforted me, touching my knee. I was deeply hurt, partly because of the mood these lyrics had brought out of me and also due to the end of a lifelong ability to always deliver the song that I had never lost, despite my disease. Now, even that had succumbed to atypical parkinsonism syndrome. My heart was broken as my family members and my pastor comforted me on the spot. Pastor Brad indicated compassionately that they had all received a gift as a result of this emotional moment. These words brought assurance that not all had been lost.

I became aware that there is a condition that accompanies multiple system atrophy, referred to in one location as "inappropriate laughing or crying." In other references, there is a term used for excessive crying as resulting from pseudobulbar affective disorder, and it is found in brain diseases such as Parkinson's or conditions resulting from brain injury. Also, deep brain stimulation surgery has been shown to result in an increase in PBA, a fact that is not lost on me as a DBS patient six months in recovery at that time after surgery.

The trigger was the emotion that was induced by the third verse. The idea of singing about dying in front of my family members altered my professional ability to focus on my song performance. It triggered an unfamiliar lack of ability to block out the crying reaction that I normally control easily while singing and playing my guitar. As my wife said, once the crying moment began, I was "off the cliff and heading down." There was no turning back. This I had never experienced before, and it had never happened while I was performing! Now, it has. I am dealing with this reality fine several days later, but deep down, my heart is broken. I will never feel that sense of musical strength that I can sing any song and deliver the message in the lyrics for my listeners—to lift, to encourage, and to bless. I lost that feeling on that Sunday. Of course, I can choose my songs carefully, and I am not overreacting, but this for me was an important marker.

Will I go on singing? I am not sure I will get back to using a voice valve to sing, but had I not had the tracheotomy, I would be performing even now. I now know that this emotional lability was always a possibility and is more so now. I won't say that the song selection was the problem, because we didn't know, based on my history, that this would happen. Now, years later, I know of my potential to go off the cliff emotionally, so I would look at each solo with care to be sure that it would not be too sensitive a subject to share on stage with my audience.

There was a silver lining in this experience. The people at Magnolia Presbyterian Church—where we had at the time been members for ten years—showed a lot of love with a standing "O" after my song with the broken performance. There was an outpouring of hugs, words of support, and kindness that was shown. Pastor Brad Copeland told me that he would welcome me to sing again without reservation. It was a special affirmation—and very much like the church we know to this day, full of loving people and leaders who care. Throughout my experience with atypical parkinsonism, they have been there for our family and supported me as a musician, as well. We are always grateful for our Magnolia Presbyterian Church Family!

Adjusting with the Support of Others

As time went along, Karrie and I found other ways to adjust. After the loss of our two pets, Chester the black cat and Jamaica the Labrador retriever, we didn't have the same need for a yard. We decided to downsize and sold the house we had been in for nine years after the start of my neurological disease. We were successful in buying a home near our church, doctors, hospitals, and nursing homes in which I sang with my friend, Les. It was a one-story home in a secure, gated community in an area of Riverside along a scenic drive well known in the area. We had just enough room and a tiny yard with less to care for, but many services around the common areas were taken care of by the homeowners association. We have settled for the last time.

During this time living in Riverside, we began to visit nursing homes in the area. First, my friend Gary Edwards introduced me to a place nearby where I could go on to play and sing twice each month. Gary got me started, and whenever he flew into town, he drove me there, and we sang together. The weeks that Gary was not there, Karrie always drove us. After several month, Les Racadio would join us with his wife, Maggie. Les is a wonderfully skilled guitarist and he provided accompaniment for me for five years as we visited the patients. We played a great variety of recognizable songs by Glen Campbell, Albert King, Robert Johnson, Kenny Rogers, Johnny Cash, John Denver, and Neil Diamond, just to name a few, in addition to gospel and Christian tunes we would share. We enjoyed these times with Les and Maggie, playing and singing and having lunch together.

We added two more nursing homes for another year, with Karrie playing percussion instruments with me. She was not only my rhythm section but my driver and roadie who helped carry my guitar or mandolin. I really enjoyed getting to provide entertainment and inspiration through music at these nursing facilities. These were people whom I could relate to, as well as they could relate to me. Their eyes would grow large when I told them my story about brain surgery and a rare form of Parkinson's that made playing and singing harder, but I wouldn't quit regardless of how my skills might decay.

We were moving along with our lives, doing what we could, though I was limited in my abilities to walk, requiring a walker or cane and driving was something I had given up completely in 2006. So, for the most part, our times out and away were limited to church, doctor's appointments, singing for the patients, and an occasional coffee shop for breakfast or lunch. I will always cherish these times Karrie and I spent together going out to eat and spending time talking and laughing. I wasn't well, but I was strong inside and determined to appreciate what we still had: us. Being together. Our great family, who love each other and care and always do their best to pitch in and support their parents with whatever is going on.

During the year leading up to my breathing emergency on January 3, 2020, I had three special visits from friends that were particularly noteworthy. Five classmates from our years growing up in the schools in Lakewood made a special trip to come and see me. These were guys I had known since we were in the early grades of elementary school and on through high school. They cared enough to gather together and drive the sixty miles to our home out in Riverside, just to sit with me and talk a few hours. We had a great time, so great that I wrote a song about their visit called "Vader Tavern." Ed Alvarado, Jerry Egherman, Roger Baker, Mike Taibi, and Dave Worts had once sat beside me in class as boys, and here they were in my living room. Mike Taibi and Ed Alvarado have stayed in touch, following up on our progress from time to time. I am so grateful.

"Vader Tavern" by Daniel Brooks
(Can be heard on YouTube on Danstune's Channel)
One day I stopped into Vader Tavern, where
my friends were all gathered round
They looked me up and gave an invitation,
come to the tavern and drink one down.

We were young when met, we just couldn't forget
We are friends to this day, as I sing this song
Though our lives have traveled on.

So good to see my childhood friends,
let's get together before the end
Ed, Jerry, Roger, Mike and Dave, just
didn't know which friend to save.

We were young at the start, it was an act of the heart
We were friends at that time, now I want to say
I will need their help one day.

Another visitor was Michael Healey, who came to see us shortly after the guys from the old neighborhood. Mike and I had been friends since our first year at Long Beach City College. He visited one Saturday for a good long time, and we played instruments together, talking, reminiscing, and telling each other stories. Karrie made us a nice dinner, and we had a really nice day of it, really thinking back on our memories of younger years. I appreciated that effort he made.

Peggy Thomas was a friend from my career days. We worked together at three schools, where I was an administrator. She was my right-hand organizer and facilitator of special projects, so we had an important working relationship. She had known Karrie since 1989 also, so we were longtime friends.

Peggy was coming out from Florida to go to her fiftieth high school reunion. So she contacted me, knowing I was struggling with my illness, and scheduled a time to come by. We had a nice hour-long visit. Peggy and I talked about the days at school and programs we had put together as a team. My sister, Teri, was staying with us for a few days, so she also was able to meet her. We had a very nice visit, and I am thankful for friends like Peggy, who cared to take the time and come on by. Little did we know that, in a few short months, I would be having a tracheotomy and a feeding tube insertion. Also, the pandemic would be right around the corner, and our ability to see people was about to become very limited.

When I was facing the life I was left to live as a patient with a trach and feeding tube and going through the two months in the hospital, I reflected frequently on how fortunate I was to have such great friends.

Individuals who would take time to go see a sick friend in need and bring some cheer. Who knows? I may not have made it through those hours of crisis, and it would have been a wonderful last year to get the chance to spend time with dear people that I cherished knowing. They did what their hearts told them, and for that, I am eternally grateful.

CHAPTER SEVEN

Tracheostomy and Feeding Tube

I have so much to share, but it is not within my power to write all that has occurred. I have long known that my vocal cords, swallowing, and breathing risk were big issues with the autonomic failure of MSA. On January 3, 2020, I had a breathing crisis and was rushed to the hospital. While there, I struggled until I was near the end. Karrie helped inform the doctors and nurses of the type of disease I have, and they saved my life. I was under heavy sedation and on a ventilator for five days—while the family didn't know the shape I would be in, even if I were brought back.

I applaud Karrie and the wonderful physicians at Riverview Community Hospital, who determined that a tracheostomy tube inserted in my trachea and a PEG feeding tube placed through my torso into my stomach were my best chance of survival and preventing the same breathing crisis from recurring. At the time of the writing these three paragraphs, I was in my bed recuperating at Compassionate Care Nursing Home, and with the help of experts, I was learning to use a trach permanently, along with the gastric feeding (liquid only) situation. Family training is involved, and my sons, their wives, and our grandkids have all been so supportive. Thanks to all of our closest family, friends, and church, who have sent love and prayers our way. Karrie never missed a day of my long hospital stay, and our sons, Daniel, Mark, and Stephen, brought their families to visit several times. My brother Matt, my sister Teri, my nieces, Leah and Lindi, and my son Mark's father-in-law, Bill, all visited me during this time. Matt and his fiancé, Lillian, were there to visit me at Compassionate Care Nursing Home a number of times during my rehab. While at the hospital where I had the major surgeries and an eleven day stay, two of my longtime friends visited, Jerry Ricketts and David Collier. David came nearly every day of the eleven, which I will always appreciate. Also, our pastors, Claire and Paul, came to support us. I am so thankful to all of you!

I am alive by the grace of God, the miracle of science, and dedicated medical professionals. Thank you most sincerely. During that difficult period, I missed my sweetheart, who as I have stated, visited me every single day. We will go on in mutual love and shared faith. Karrie and I would not have pulled through without our great—and I mean great—sons, their wives, and our grandkids. Many cards and texts were sent by family and lifelong friends, which meant so much. I received several cards each week from my mother-in-law, Mary Lou Hynick, and her husband, Jim. Karrie's mother has taken over all mom "needs" since the sudden passing of our beloved mother, Marguerite, in 2017. Mary Lou is so dearly loved. January 3, 2020 was a day that changed life as we knew it forever. I arrived at the emergency room struggling to get a breath, and the medical professionals went right to work trying to restore an airway. As they were attempting to save my life and I was on the brink of oxygen deprivation, I looked at Karrie's loving and concerned face one last time, and she looked at mine.

Since I could not move a single finger or move my mouth to speak, I hoped somehow my eyes would show my need for help and she could convey this to the emergency-room staff. Somehow she knew, and when she said, "He can't get air," they put a large instrument down my throat and then an intubation tube. Next, I went to ICU, and discussions ensued.

Karrie and my soon-to-be surgeon were discussing the conditions that caused my vocal cord paralysis. From Karrie's explanation, he knew exactly what multiple system atrophy was and how it could stop the body's ability to get proper signals from the brain, thus interfering with a person's ability to breathe. Thank God for this doctor, for whom it all clicked. Also, my own ENT doctor came to see about the situation and contributed a good deal of information about my brain disease and its effects on my vocal cords. It was determined that the best route would be a tracheostomy, as well as a feeding PEG tube, inserted directly in my stomach through my torso in order to prevent the future reoccurrence of the inability to get oxygen or choking on food and liquid, which I had been experiencing severely for years.

As I was then put under heavy anesthesia, a measure to keep me safe from removing any tubing, I was put on a ventilator. Then I waited out the weekend for a three day stretch before I could be operated on. The surgeon opened a hole in my trachea and inserted a tracheostomy tube. During this time, I neither saw, nor was I aware, of much of anything occurring around me. I was fighting for life and at times had to be restrained because I unconsciously would attempt to pull out what to me were foreign objects from my mouth.

I had pneumonia and a high fever following my two simultaneous operations, the trach, and the feeding tube insertion into my stomach. I contracted a staph infection, and they had to check my heart function, which through all of this was doing great. My sons, our daughters-in-law, Karrie, and my brother and his fiancé all hoped that, when I made it out of all this, I would still be me and have my full capacities. As I have said, several close friends came by during my hospitalization, for which I am deeply appreciative.

Some great doctors, nurses, and staff performed and decided on so many best practices that led to my successful surgeries. Now I had my trach in place and my PEG tube, but I wouldn't be finished fighting.

Next, I will tell you about my dream state from anesthesia, as well as the delusions that followed me for weeks until the medicine worked its way out of my body. Also, a few weeks later, while at the rehab hospital, I had to be sent out twice to a nearby hospital to have my dislodged PEG tube replaced through surgery.

I must add that I had no idea how much my family went through until weeks later, when through many conversations, they helped me sort out my dreams from the reality of what actually happened. I don't write this account lightly, assuming it's hard for my dear ones to relive. They went through so much worry, wondering if they had lost me. I am so very thankful for all who stood by me, especially Karrie and our beautiful family.

After the emergency, during the days leading up to the surgery, I was heavily medicated, so I was unaware of my surroundings in the intensive care unit. Then, after the tracheostomy surgery was planned, Karrie communicated with the neurologist that I had talked with her in the past about a PEG feeding tube, should the need ever arise. The PEG tube would be inserted to avoid the risks associated with eating and choking that could lead to pneumonia because of the lack of coordination between my brain and the poorly working mechanisms in my throat. I had been choking for years, and it was time to try to prevent this same emergency from reoccurring. Karrie insisted that I not have to go through two separate operations, and the surgeons agreed to work together—making the incision to open a passageway in my throat and another in my abdomen to enter my stomach. These operations resulted in two prosthetic devices, a trach tube, and a PEG tube, as permanent additions to my body for sustaining my life in the future. After these operations took place three days after my breathing crisis, there were four to five days post-surgery in ICU, for which I was nearly out most of the time, and I have no memory of much of what was occurring.

I eventually regained consciousness and awareness, but even then it was limited. There was a period of a few days where the neurologist was checking several times each day to see if I was coming around. It wasn't clear whether I would return to my personality and existence as a person who knew what and who I was. My right side seemed to not work, and there were concerns that, during a time of oxygen deprivation, I might possibly have had neurological changes that debilitated my conscious mind in some manner. Also, it wasn't clear if I would regain the movement of my limbs, particularly on my right side. My left hand seemed to be working better than the right arm and leg, as I would reach up and try to disconnect the ventilator tube, which had originally been connected to the intubation tube, but after the surgery, was connected directly to my tracheostomy tube. I seemed to struggle a lot to get free, so during my stay in the hospital, I often had a nursing attendant near my bed, ready to stop me from trying to take my tube off of my trach with my left hand.

At times, when there were less people at night, the staff would restrain my left arm by tying it to the bed, preventing me from doing something that would cause damage. I have small flashes of time that I can recall that involve stories I developed in my mind combined with dreams. One or two involve the restraints and the memory of being held against my will in another place entirely, not in the hospital. The restraints had a big effect on my psyche, and though I understand this was needed, it was also traumatizing while being medicated with narcotics to keep me from harming myself. Because of the strong medicines I was receiving, I had delusional experiences that seemed real and stay with me to this day. I have a form of deja vu that I can't shake yet, but it is getting better.

When I began to come around after about six days, they had to determine if I could breathe without the ventilator. I was weaned off of this machine gradually, a little more each time they would attempt it. There would be a reaction, and I would seemingly panic, and they would have to medicate me once more to prevent trauma or lack of breathing. Eventually, I was able to be taken off the ventilator and breathe on my own with oxygen being provided through a trach mask. At that point, I was moved to another kind of room called a direct observation unit.

I had various staff, including nursing assistants and nurses, not to mention the respiratory therapists that enter into several delusional stories I developed. I would think that I was in another world, at a coffee shop, or with my family or my wife, free from the hospital environment. I thought I was being held against my will and insisted that they let me go or contact my wife. I felt paranoid that various staff had it in for me, that they were making fun of me for having on a gown and not staying covered up appropriately. I remember trying to get up, which would have resulted in my falling, and they would put my legs and feet back on the bed. Soon after, I would again put my feet on the floor and insist that Karrie was waiting for me outside in the car.

When I wanted to talk with my wife, I would call her in my mind, at least I thought. I figured that phones were wireless, and therefore, I could dial home and (what one doctor told me months later was a perception that I had a built in Bluetooth) leave Karrie a message. When she came each day, I would ask, "Why didn't you return my phone calls?"

She would reply patiently, "I didn't know there was a message," even though I had no phone with me or at my bedside. I would tell my wife, Karrie, about these incidents that I perceived involving staff misbehavior and let her know about the mean and crazy sounding things that happened while she was home.

She would listen patiently to me and do all she could to calm my concerns and fears. She even acted on my complaints at one point, going to the registered nurse in charge of my case and expressing her concern about what I thought staff members had done to persecute me. God bless her for always believing in me and doing all she could to try to correct a situation that was overwhelmingly in my head or imagination, induced by a deeply sedated state of mind and from being in ICU. For a week or two, I don't even think I realized that I had a trach or a PEG tube at all.

After eleven days in the hospital, I was transferred to a post-acute skilled nursing facility, Compassionate Care, to rehabilitate. This move took place the night that our son, Daniel, had his birthday. He stopped by on the way home from work and checked on me. Later, the administration sent someone to let me know that they had found a place in a nearby facility that had a bed for me, as well as the capability among staff to care for my trach and PEG tube feeding needs. I perceived this as an award that I was getting for being able to use a device called a Passy Muir valve to talk. I thought that I was receiving a scholarship to a special rehabilitation camp or school, where an entire group like me, with tracheostomies, would have rest, training, scenic gardens, and fireside inspirational chats. I had no idea that I was going to a nursing home, though to others around me this was a clear conclusion.

A nursing home is a very good thing for a person in the condition that I was in, but it is also an awful thing because some of the patients can be annoying or scary. A lot of noise, interruptions, and bad behavior by patients is both threatening and alarming. I remember arriving there the night of our son's birthday, and I wanted to go to the bathroom. I hadn't realized that I had a catheter attached to my privates and had been urinating directly into a bag twenty-four hours a day for two weeks by then. I stood up precariously and, with my weakened legs and parkinsonian walking condition, attempted to head toward the bathroom. I was interrupted by an angry voice. "Get back in that bed! You don't get up from that bed!"

She was shouting, and I perceived that I was being thought of as a rebel and was being treated like a bad boy at school. She went to get a tall man who came in to strong arm me, figuratively speaking. He said, "What seems to be the problem?"

I replied, "I am not wanting to be oppositional in any way. I just want to know how to use the bathroom." He convinced me to get back in bed and forget about it.

I did, and two hours later, much to my horror, I had a big accident where I went number two on the bed and made a huge mess. I didn't know what to do and felt frightened and humiliated. I took my bedding and tried to clean everything up. An LVN, a gentleman who was so kind, came by, smelling my odiferous waste. He called for his nursing assistant; they were called CNAs, and the two of them patiently cleaned me up and took away all the dirty bedding. Being changed like a baby was hard to get used to once I was alert and aware of my surroundings. For weeks, I began to wish for the day I could rise from the bed and walk to the bathroom and relieve myself without any help.

One night, after I was at the SNF for about three weeks, I accidentally removed my PEG tube. I kneeled on the top of my bed to get situated, and when I did, I accidentally yanked my tube right through my abdomen. It was completely dislodged as I bled from this open wound. This was the day that one of my favorite athletes, Kobe Bryant, had died with his daughter and her friends in a fiery crash in a helicopter. A bad day all around ended with my own serious situation. The staff attempted to replace the PEG tube, but with no success. I was sent by ambulance to a local hospital emergency room. My wife, Karrie, met me and waited with me and our son, Mark, for the time when, hours later, the doctor would do a procedure, without anesthesia, to replace the tube in my stomach. It seemed to be successful, and the EMTs took me back to my bed at the nursing home.

The next night, when the LVN was putting my meds into my PEG tube (nothing was entering my mouth, so both nutrition and medications had to be placed with a syringe in my stomach through the PEG tube), the medicine started spilling out of my stoma and onto my abdomen. She said, "Oh, no! Something's wrong!" The tube, placed the night before in the emergency room, had not remained properly in my stomach, and the medicine was now pouring out of me. This meant there was another emergency. I was again taken by ambulance to the emergency room to have it replaced. This time, they realized it wasn't advisable to do this again without admitting me to the hospital and doing surgery two days later. I was put "under," and a very skillful surgeon placed it correctly where it has remained to this day.

While at Compassionate Care Nursing Home, I was in a room with another bed, so I had three different roommates during my six-week stay. One was there three weeks, another for only five days, and the last roomie lasted the final two weeks I was there and continued beyond my time. The first roommate was a hard-working patient, determined to get home. He put his heart into the physical therapy opportunity they provided and inspired me to do the same. I became aware that my desire to leave the nursing home was only going to play out if the professional staff viewed my fitness, physically, mentally and medically, as being adequate enough for me to function safely within our own home. My roommate, Ron, who was in the bed next to mine when I checked in on January 14, had a breathing emergency too, leading to his rehab. He had a trach, which was removed at some point, since his had been strictly for emergency purposes.

Ron was receiving trays of food and drink three times each day, something I had to get used to being around, not being allowed to eat or drink anything. These trays of savory-smelling hospital cafeteria delights, which I rarely had a glimpse of, were brought on full plates and removed by staff, half eaten on a seemingly endless hamster wheel. I was getting thirsty and hungry after several weeks without a drop of water in my mouth and nothing that resembled food entering my stomach.

My second roommate, Bill, was in his eighties and came after a severe heart attack and several comorbidities, including diabetes and kidney disease. This poor old fellow was dying the day he was admitted and cried out in pain, murmuring requests throughout the day and night. He was struggling to exist, and it was heart-wrenching to see him taken at 4:00 a.m. each day to leave the facility and be transported to a hospital where his insurance covered dialysis. His exit required a ride in a Hoyer lift, upon which he would hang precariously like a wounded animal, suspended in animation as he whimpered in pain. I felt for old Bill and tried to be friendly. The fifth day, our son, Daniel, was there hanging out with me at my bedside. Bill wanted Daniel to help him contact his family, which he did. They dialed, and he reached a family member to speak briefly, seemingly begging them to come and see him one last time. Soon, I would find out why.

Daniel left that afternoon to go and celebrate Karrie's birthday, and within twenty minutes, Bill had passed. Thank God Daniel had been there to kindly assist this fellow patient to phone his wife and daughter. He lay there beside me for several hours before they did finally come and take him under a shroud, out on a stretcher. A sobering reminder of the delicate nature of our lives.

My third roommate was a wonderful guy, Gustavo, who spoke no English but said, within minutes of meeting me, that we were, "Simpatico." We certainly did hit it off, and I spent quite a bit of time using my iPhone, looking up words and phrases in English to translate them into Spanish, something I became a bit better at as the two weeks progressed. We took turns watching English and Spanish channels. Though Gustavo wouldn't insist on it, I encouraged him to take the remote and enjoy whatever he preferred. He was humble and kind. We looked out for each other. He had been injured traumatically in a car accident and had a head injury. His throat had been compromised, and he was required to have a tracheostomy for a period of several months. When he was moved to my room, he had been decannulated and was learning to breath without the trach. When he needed meds, he would stumble over to the door with his feeding tube hanging out from under his shirt like a loose rope swinging from an unmoored ship. He would do this several times each day, impatiently waiting for the next dose to give him relief from pain, or boredom or both. He was a very good guy, and we were simpatico, indeed.

Ron was busy getting in shape and talking about going home. I realized, in those first few weeks, that I had better get interested and motivated to head down the long hall for physical therapy if I ever hoped to take my trach and feeding tube home to live in relative freedom. I had a few wonderful occupational and physical therapists who devoted themselves to helping all of us. Each day, Monday through Friday, I spent a minimum of one hour working hard on my arms, legs, fingers, and aerobic fitness. These workouts included great—if not at times, laborious—conversations, which added to the color of my seemingly endless days. Rosita was cheerful and energetic, while Edith worked with me on my dexterity and occupational needs. Ross led me in my strengthening and walking regimen. This gentleman enjoyed the birds that visited outside the window of the physical therapy room, and was particularly friendly and helpful. He was a spiritual man, and we had much to talk about as he would hold my gait belt, guiding me carefully as I learned, again, to walk slowly while supported by a walker. It wasn't clear that I would walk easily enough to leave the hospital until several weeks had passed. I kept hoping that I would appear able to move and be balanced enough to avoid falls so that they would eventually release me.

I felt paranoid. I was unsure why I was there and why I couldn't leave. No doubt, I had experienced a very difficult stay in the previous hospital, and I couldn't remember much of that time. I had been there at Riverview Community Hospital for eleven days, most of which were a blur of scary and weird moments. I wasn't even fully aware of the trach and the feeding tube until several days after I was at Compassionate Care Nursing Home. They were equipped to handle post-acute patients with tracheostomies and feeding tubes. The nurses were well versed in how to feed me through my abdomen, which they did with the use of a feeding machine that slowly pumped what I called my "peanut butter shake" that was my liquid food. There was no taste, but there would come a somewhat satisfying fullness at the conclusion of the day. This feeding was constant and deliberately slow as my stomach developed the ability to accept this gravity feeding process.

There were IVs attached to me to ward off the insidious infections I developed, first in the hospital when I had pneumonia and MURSA. I also had developed an infection in my arm that caused it to swelled up a third larger due to a blockage in the main artery that runs through my arm, leading to my vital organs. This problem was to return with the IV that I received at Compassionate Care to complete the course of antibiotics meant to hopefully extinguish the infections I had developed. My arm began to hurt badly, and I would feel painful pressure in the shoulder area. This bothered my nurses, and they sought a physician to determine if this was a serious concern and how to remedy it.

They decided to move the IV to my left arm and my veins. By this time, they were almost impenetrable and rolled over as they poked feverishly at my forearm, wrist and hand, hoping to strike gold. It took three individual nurses until a lead registered nurse was able to shave enough hair and get a clear target. She made it look easy and wondered at all the poking and prodding that had taken place.

Through it all, Karrie drove to Compassionate Care to see me all forty-four days. It was an hour's drive, particularly in the evening commuter traffic, common to our region that is filled with folks who work remotely from our bedroom communities. Karrie was dedicated to my comfort and was a big help to the staff. She would visit daily, from 9:00 a.m. through 4:00 p.m., until we got wise and realized that, if she left by 3:00 p.m. each day, she would have a much better trip home, cutting it from ninety to forty minutes.

I can't emphasize enough how much Karrie's companionship meant. So few patients had this kind of company and to this degree. I was the luckiest man in that home, and it was apparent to all the staff that I had an advocate and an understanding family member who showed grace and appreciation to the professionals that served so faithfully. After a few days, Karrie made a request to have a medical team meeting on my behalf. She politely demanded this meeting, and they obliged. She was able to discuss with the various department heads from nursing, social work, business, respiratory therapy, and medical offices what my prognosis was and what my stay would be like in treatment and length.

Karrie left that meeting, unbeknownst to me, a bit worried about how soon, if ever, I would get to leave that facility. The brain diseases I had—called multiple system atrophy, along with corticobasal syndrome—were enough of a challenge. However, the neurological damage that may have occurred in the emergency breathing episode and the two prosthetics that resulted were enough to give an early impression that I may need full-time medical staff care around the clock for the rest of my life. Karrie didn't want to shatter my hope of leaving and kindly kept these concerns to herself. Meanwhile, she was optimistically preparing our home for my return. She ordered me a great big, new recliner that raised the feet and lowered the back just by pushing buttons. She got the hospital bed in place and ordered the bedding and pads to go on it. She moved furniture and lovingly planned the safest paths and environment that our home would allow. All she did during this time was hopefully and prayerfully work toward my return.

Meanwhile, I think her heart was broken. She went home to an empty house for fifty-five days. We hadn't been apart more than a few nights at a time, and only for work related conferences and student activities for our thirty-eight years of marriage. We were inseparable, and I felt badly that my sweet partner and wife went home to an empty house every day for those eight weeks that felt like six months.

Compassionate Care was a nursing facility that had a great staff. I had several really caring and dedicated nurses and nursing assistants that cared for me. I depended on their visits and genuine interest in my wellbeing. The doctors I saw infrequently were knowledgeable and took an interest in what was happening with my medical situation. The maintenance staff was kind and kept the rooms neat and clean. Our physical therapy team were friendly and devoted to getting us in shape and ready to go home in a safe and successful manner. Most importantly, there were respiratory therapists who were essential to the care I needed with a new tracheostomy.

I saw as many as a dozen different respiratory therapists, with several being particularly helpful to me in my recovery effort. They were there day and night to check on my breathing and the safety of my trach, to ensure that it was in place and that my oxygen intake was being maintained at a healthy level. They had me on oxygen through a tracheostomy mask for the first month or more, up until the second procedure I had at a hospital near Compassionate Care to surgically re-insert my PEG tube into a new location through my abdomen. When I returned from that surgery, they had saved my room for me, and I no longer seemed to need constant oxygen, so that process was ended.

The nebulizer treatments occurred a few times every twenty-four hours and opened up my lungs and bronchial tubes to allow more circulation of oxygen so that my body could receive its benefits, as they were needed to maintain my vital health. This process was about a fifteen-minute proposition. My tracheostomy mask was attached to a flexible tube that brought a rescue medicine to my trach, and thus it entered my pulmonary system to dilate the lung tissue to increase its capacity and efficacy. The respiratory therapist would change my inner cannula and clean the tissue around my trach at least once per day and would check my oximeter reading for the percentage of oxygen in my blood stream.

There were staff members who took care of the feeding machine that was pumping liquid food directly into my stomach twenty-four hours a day. They also made sure I had intravenous antibiotic treatments for the various infections I brought with me from the hospital, and the infections were treated, thoroughly. By the time I left Compassionate Care, there were no more IVs needed for use at home.

Our grown children all wished to answer the call to be trained in how to care for my tracheostomy when I would go home. In the end, Mark, whose wife was expecting a baby in the near future, signed up to join Karrie for the day-long training. This required Mark to get the day off from work. I will always appreciate the time Mark and Karrie spent in that class with me and the courage it took for them to employ the training by doing the actual trach cleaning and cannula changes for me, which were needed in order to be certified. Karrie went on for days, helping and learning more each day, skills and knowledge that are paying off greatly today.

I was in the hospital eleven days and in the nursing home six weeks. I didn't know what to expect when I got home, though Karrie did so much to prepare the way for me. Our home is set up so well, with a hospital bed, the IV pole for the feedings through my tube, and a cart for the tracheostomy supplies. Karrie is so organized! We moved some guitars and mandolins out of our second-bedroom closet, and Karrie made a storage area for the boxes of liquid food, trach supplies, and a bunch of materials!

By the seventh week home, we were adjusting well. Karrie has the trach care down, as well as the feeding process. The trach requires an a.m. and p.m. servicing. She does the following:

Morning: She removes debris from around the stoma (hole in my throat), removes and replaces the inner cannula, suctions the trachea as needed, and removes and replaces the trach tie that holds it on my neck. She cleans the area around my stomach tube (PEG) with a Q tip and saline water.

Evening: She removes debris from around the stoma, suctions the trachea as needed.

Monthly: The actual trach tube that holds the inner cannula has to be completely replaced. Our ENT doctor does this, but the last time we went, he trained Karrie, and she removed and replaced my tracheostomy tube, which is daunting! She did it well and, within the next few months, took over the task. It means taking the old one out, which leaves just the open hole in my throat—and then she puts a tiny bit of lube on the tip and carefully guides it in, while exerting some pressure. This process is mildly uncomfortable, but I am used to it now, having had it replaced many times. It was one of my biggest hurdles, but I feel confident today about this process. It is something you can't "take your time" with because the opening in my throat will close itself after a while. We need to get right on it once we take out the worn trach, or I could have trouble breathing.

With regard to feeding, there is nothing by mouth—and here is the process: Three times per day, Karrie hangs a bag on the IV pole with a tube for attaching to my stomach tube that has a valve on it—which closes and opens. She fills the bag with 700 calories of liquid (looks like a peanut butter shake) and then opens the valve at the bottom on the bag, and it drips into my stomach for forty minutes. At the conclusion of each feeding, she uses a large syringe to pour medications that have been crushed and mixed with water, into my stomach tube. Finally, she pushes the syringe with clear water, and it removes the leftover food and liquid, putting it in my stomach.

These processes are time consuming, and we are very much homebodies, with or without COVID-19. We will always have these things to do.

I am a trach patient, and this on top of the fact that I have an atypical parkinsonism condition called multiple system atrophy. I still have movement difficulties, such as tremors and walking struggles, in addition to all the autonomic issues I have, including drops in blood pressure called orthostatic hypotension. My second-month home, I had the deep brain stimulator *generator* replaced in my chest. This system, which sends a flow of electricity into my deep brain in two places through implants, is still very helpful to me, and I have had this now nine years!

This whole new way of life is hard to get used to, but like one of my friends told me, "It's your new normal." I am still human, and I fear the shortening of my life. I have greater faith than ever that my life is in Christ and that he has plans for me on this earth. I was saved from dying on January 3rd, 2020, and I am so grateful for God's grace extended through the doctors, the nurses, staff, and of course, my wonderful wife and sons, who supported me, along with their great spouses, who are like daughters. Our grandkids sent me pictures and letters, which lifted my spirits greatly. Many friends and family prayed for us and continue to do so. Thank you!

Being home but isolated due to COVID-19 has been very trying. It is worth living, having the feeding tube and trach, and while some reject them, I chose life. I had talked to Karrie about the possible need for these measures many times before my emergency, and she knew I preferred to live on, especially because of our family and sweet grand kids. They are my purpose now. I still play my instruments, but singing causes pain in my throat, so I am trying to limit it to a minimum. This is a great loss for me.

I didn't think I could sing with a tracheostomy, but I did on a limited basis for a few months when I returned home. I have a Passy Muir speaking valve, which allows air in through my tracheostomy, but exhaling requires it to travel past my vocal cords. Without this I cannot sing, while with it I can sing a bit. My first video performance at church was a rendition of "Give Me Jesus" by Fernando Ortega. This was my first performance since having a "trach" put it in. The need for my tracheostomy results from partial but progressive vocal cord paralysis. Also, my swallowing problem causes food and drinks to slip into my lungs, so now I eat through a tube in my stomach. These conditions result from multiple system atrophy, and as I have explained, this is an atypical parkinsonism syndrome. Of late, I am not singing much, and after a recent adjustment to the type of trach I use, I will likely no longer be singing much at all. I will explain this more in a later chapter.

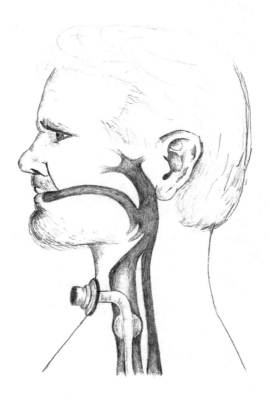

Cuffed Tracheostomy Tube

CHAPTER EIGHT

A New Normal

My friend Pat, on the Mandolin Cafe forum, had his class praying for me in a Florida high school. I had gotten to know him over the years since I had developed my love for playing and collecting mandolins. We often talk and reflect on our mandolin interests, playing styles, goals for acquisition of mandolins, and other various common interests, such as educating young minds and school related matters. Pat had kept up with my story during these seven years I had been online with the Mandolin Cafe forum. His interest has been keen, and when his sons' high school became the epicenter of the Valentine's Day high school shooting tragedy, I felt such a sense of concern and despair over this incident and how it escalated the ever growing number of such cases of school shootings. We commiserated about this, and I have kept his sons in mind as they have proceeded to matriculate through that school, and I wondered what it would have been like to be in his shoes as a father. Pat is a great guy with a very special outlook on life and a deep understanding of high school English curriculum and preparing promising young minds for a successful future in letters.

After I was home with the tracheostomy and the PEG tube for feeding, I was updating my friend Pat about these changes and how I was working at finding my way through daily life: a life without food taken by mouth and breathing through a very fancy hole in my neck.

He said, "You will go on being you, just you with a new normal." I so appreciated this explanation because I wasn't sure how to put it into words. I only knew that I was feeling the disappointment of the loss of freedom to leave the house, the fear of dying an early death, and concern about all the work and trouble I was bringing to my wife, who was assuming responsibility for all of my care. "You'll still be you, just you with a new normal way of being," I thought. It helped to keep this thought in mind as I move forward, and I would tell Pat, if I could see him in person one day, that I appreciated his encouragement and the way he helped me define this.

Each day I wake up with a sense that life is different, that I am physically different, and that things will never be the same. In the morning, I am full of hope and energy, thinking of playing an instrument, whether electric blues guitar, acoustic folk rock music, recording a video to add to the church's online worship, and one of my mandolins which is my favorite hobby—the mandolin. I do indeed have a lot of interests and things to do, though I do not drive, and the COVID-19 pandemic is causing the shelter-in-place lifestyle. Karrie and I are at home constantly, with only a few small exceptions, when we run out to drop something at the post office or UPS Store. Finding ways to spend time is a challenge, even with my interests in music, reading, and communicating online, while Karrie is doing stitchery, puzzle books, reading, or paper arts. I am always impressed with her creations, including greeting cards and photo albums. Our family memories are well preserved in colorfully displayed albums with captions and graphics affixed to pages of photos laid out in thematic designs.

In the evening, the degenerative brain disease takes a toll on me, and as the sun goes down, I get depressed. It is known as sundowner syndrome, and it is persistent. Karrie knows how to help me through this, and we are able to make the adjustments through sharing a laugh with light comedy programs and some medications that are beneficial. The night is hardest with these atypical parkinsonism conditions, emotionally and physically.

The tracheostomy took getting used to, of course. There was irritation, pain, fear, and anxiety. The feeding tube was a huge adjustment, with simply the lack of eating on any regular basis or any significant foods. Favorite foods were out—no pancakes, burritos, tacos, pizza, French fries, or cooked breakfast. The idea of ever barbecuing again was out. We got rid of the new barbecue we had purchased just a couple of years earlier. Getting accustomed to changing the trach each month, which was scary at first, gradually became easier. Initially, we went to the ear, nose, throat physician to have it switched out. He has it down to an art! He did it once and then showed Karrie how to take one out and put in a new trach. I will provide an illustration for how this looks in place and also tell you that the technique Karrie learned was excellently employed and her skill in doing so has gotten better and better. I have so much trust in her putting my tracheostomy tube in that she is my preferred person to ever change the typical trach we used this first year (a Portex size 8, uncuffed).

Then I had the second breathing emergency. This came in October of 2020, ten months after the initial crisis on January 3, which led to my present situation. One night in October 2020, I was struggling to get air through my trach. It wasn't resolving, and Karrie decided to try suctioning my trach to see if she could get down past it and clear whatever was constricting my windpipe. When she went down the tracheostomy tube to suction, it made getting any air more impossible. I was wheezing beyond wheezing, and my heart rate dropped down into the twenty-five beats per minute range on the oximeter. By the time Karrie saw the reading on my heart rate, she had already called the ambulance. The EMTs arrived and bagged me (a process with a bag that is squeezed at a regular rate to manually force air in and out to keep me breathing). I was bagged all the way the emergency room, where they suctioned and treated me for twenty-four hours, as I have described in another section of this book. I was tested for several things related to blood gases, my heart, and my lungs, and I had a CT with radioactive isotope in my bloodstream to determine how my lungs were functioning. Coming home meant more new normals.

From October until present, I required oxygen nearly 100 percent of the day, with the ability to be away from it for short portions to brush my teeth or go for a short ride to get a coffee at a drive-through Starbucks near our home. With this oxygen came the realization that the doctors had found that my lungs were not functioning anywhere near 100 percent, with a portion of each debilitated from damage in the past. When hospitalized in January of 2020, I had pneumonia very severely, and it may have left damage. We do know that there is evidence of a large portion of my right lung that is not functioning, and the right side of my diaphragm is not lifting as it should to rhythmically push my right lung to inhale and exhale. This was a factor of my neurodegenerative disease. In other words, my brain was not sending signals to my diaphragm to work, and it was gradually losing its abilities. My life was going in the wrong direction, but I was still looking up, with hopeful expectation that I could make the best of these circumstances.

We went to see our pulmonologist, Dr. Ivan Sproll, who had a keen interest in my case. He was the surgeon who conducted the operation to put the tracheostomy tube in on January 7, 2020. He explained how neuro-muscular diseases affect the breathing structures in our bodies and let us know the difficult news that I was going to be better off using a ventilator in the near fu-ture. He wanted to schedule a procedure a month later, which would have fallen during the winter holidays of 2020, but COVID-19 had filled all the beds in the lo-cal hospitals, and it was put off until March 2021.

On March 16, 2021, I went into Riverview Community Hospital to have a cuffed trach put in my stoma that would enable a complete seal of the airway. The cuffed trach is used for patients who need to be on a ventilator. It is a different device than the smooth version that I was using, an uncuffed Portex number 8. When this task was completed, I would be sent home, and eventually the equipment would arrive, and Karrie would be trained in how to inflate and deflate my cuffed trach made by Shiley. She would also have train-ing in the operation of a ventilator, and I would initial-ly use this each night as I slept to enable my lungs to get a more optimal expansion to keep them as healthy as possible and to compensate for the lack of strength and movement in my diaphragm.

The procedure was a bit more strenuous than I had thought because the Shiley size was a different specification than the Portex. Dr. Sproll used a bronchoscope to look down my windpipe and the top of my lungs where the bronchial tubes begin. He allowed me to watch as the camera patrolled the vital area of my upper airway and lungs. These structures were so interesting to see up close, and he felt that I had very clear tissue, good color, and a very healthy-looking area. I was very pleased, and so was he. He then attempted to install the Shiley, cuffed trach number 8, which in addition to the extra length and deflated balloon surrounding the tube, was a larger diameter than I was typically using with the Portex size 8. He gave it a great effort and used lidocaine sprayed into my open stoma in order to make it comfortable, if possible. He would have preferred to use a Portex cuffed trach, but there wasn't one available at Riverview Community Hospital, so we went with Shiley.

The first was larger than I was accustomed to and was painful to attempt to insert, though Dr. Sproll did so with great care. He was showing this process to Karrie by FaceTime video on the nurse's smart phone, and Karrie was watching intently. After the pain and discomfort of trying to insert what felt like a square peg into a round hole, he decided sensibly to drop down from the eight millimeter to the size 6 Shiley. This went in nicely, but when the cuff balloon was inflated, I could no longer breath in or out at all or speak. He didn't want that to situation for me, so he quickly removed that one and put a placeholder into my stoma while he waited for the respiratory therapist to find a size 7 Shiley cuffed trach, XLT, which was a longer tube than I had been using for over a year. This one went in fairly quickly, and Dr. Sproll then tested it for my breathing. In other words, if you closed off the space around the trach with a balloon, would enough air come through just the tracheostomy tube to allow me to breathe and use the ventilator when it came time to do that? It tested successfully, and the opening diameter of the size seven was large enough, and it was settled— I would go home with the cuffed Shiley number seven.

The first day was hard. I had to get over the smaller diameter, and that, coupled with the fluid that resulted from the procedure and irritation, along with the possible inflammation that would likely occur to a degree, made breathing feel like a lot of work. It gave me an anxious day and evening. I did have a fairly good night sleeping for four hours when we went to bed. I need to sleep with the hospital bed in my room raised to about forty-five degrees in order to breath well and not struggle. Kind of reminds me of the old movie *The Elephant Man*, whose main character for different reasons required partially sitting up while he slept to avoid suffocating. My case is similar, but for obviously different reasons.

It is the third day since my new cuffed trach procedure, and we have had two visits from experts, and our team is getting things lined up to help us adjust to this new lifestyle. We are going to get a very nice Trilogy ventilator and all the supplies needed for the new type of trach we are using. Karrie will be given training by the regional company we rely on to provide our equipment and supplies, as paid for by our insurance. What a blessing to live in a country where you can contribute a tax each paycheck throughout your life, and when you retire you are able to receive medical care with a very reasonable monthly fee. We are so grateful for Medicare and the Medicare advantage program, SCAN. They take such good care of us, as does our equipment and supplies provider. We are also blessed to have Tina Sanchez, our home health nurse looking out for us, and I can't forget to mention again, Rebecca Visca, my nurse practitioner with palliative care. They have both been crucial in catching problems before they worsened and referring us for medical intervention that was absolutely necessary.

I am living the new normal. I am going to keep moving further along. I will play my guitar and mandolin, read good books, listen to great music, and watch entertaining shows and sports. That's living, man! It is great to have our church community at Magnolia Presbyterian Church and all of our friends that we have found throughout our time out in the Riverside and Moreno Valley area. We are benefiting from the online church experiences we have with Magnolia, and I am gaining both new inspiration, knowledge and great friendships by participating online with the Presbyterian church up in Monterey, where my dear friend Pastor Jay Bartow and his wife, Gail, attend. Jay leads our men's small Bible study group weekly, and that really keeps me going. The online support groups are great, in particular. I attend the virtual corticobasal degeneration group led by Janet Edmondson and the multiple system atrophy online group led by Cathy Chapman and Vera James. These folks lift my spirits and share my concerns. It is a very big help.

CHAPTER NINE

Faith and Mortality

It occurred to me how much I want to be able to talk about how being farther down the road has affected my faith experience. When I say faith, I mean my own particular belief system. While it may be different from yours, some of my experiences and ideas may relate to yours and add to your own clarification of how you want to approach your own journey. Being chronically ill with a fatal disease brings many considerations to mind. As I lay on the gurney in the emergency room on January 3, 2020, I was aware that I was dying. I had reached a point where I had no ability to control the amount of oxygen I was receiving, and I had lost all control of my body. By the time the nurses were putting an intubation tube down my throat, I was paralyzed from a substance they had injected me with to prevent me from pulling the tube out or fighting their hands in the process. If I understand it right, this occurs in most cases—the fighting off of this unnatural experience.

Soon after I was intubated the first time, there was a problem with the tube getting all the way in position, thus I was not breathing well at all. I was certain I was suffocating! This followed an hour of getting very little oxygen and choking. There had already been an attempt to get me breathing by putting a mask over my mouth and nose to give me a medication to open the bronchia in the event that I was having some type of allergic reaction. After a few minutes, they ceased this because I was obviously in distress. My wife said that I wasn't having an allergy or difficulty with breathing due to any condition other than my brain disease and its effect on my vocal cords and swallowing difficulty.

Why am I recounting this detail of my medical emergency, and how does it relate to my faith? There was a moment when they needed to reintubate me. This was done successfully, but I wasn't awake to see it or know of it.

One of the best things about this near-death experience is that I thought, *I will never have to do this again. I will never have to face this moment again.* It is something I now know how to do. I had a conversation with my psychiatrist about death just a month and a half before this breathing crisis hit me. He was explaining that the moment of dying is an experience that is a part of our lives. It is a special time in a sense that is common to all people, and that moment is unique.

There is the unknown, but something really heightening occurs at that moment, regardless of faith or belief; it is common to all people. This conversation prepared me for this moment.

I would never say that near-death experiences others have described are not real. I actually have read a couple of books about such experiences that Christian people have gone through, though in my moment, I did not experience this. Often described is the vision of a bright light and an out-of-body feeling, or even a voice of God or Jesus speaking to the individual who is nearly dead. I saw and heard nothing of the kind. I was somewhat preoccupied with the moment and the worries that were rushing through my mind. It was all so quick, and yet that suffocation was so real that I wanted to rest. I was tired of the crisis and couldn't do it anymore. I had my eyes on my wonderful wife and best friend for thirty-nine years, Karrie. I could look with my eyes, but I could not speak, move, or gesture, as I have said. I wanted the folks in the room to do more and wanted them to realize I couldn't breathe.

I was there and thought, "Well, everyone has this time, and this is mine. It has arrived." In one strange way, I felt like, "This is finally happening—my moment. We all have it, and now I will finally cross this bridge and won't need to again." Somewhere in my mind, I knew that there was more to come after this moment. I was worried about Karrie, Daniel, Mark, Stephen, my daughters-in-law, and our grandchildren. I didn't want them to hurt or worry. That flashed through my mind as well. I had no other time to think. I lay there looking up at Karrie as she rubbed the top of my left hand. She said, "It's going to be okay. You're going to be all right!" I wanted to answer that I was actually leaving this world, but I could not raise my hand to mime slashing my throat in the universal gesture or make a sound. Then, the next thing I knew, I was awake a week later, off and on—with a tracheostomy tube in my throat and a feeding tube in my stomach.

A result of this whole experience, including the ensuing eleven days in the hospital, followed by six weeks in a nursing home, was that I was determined to be more aware and intentional about fostering my faith walk. I determined that my life had been saved because of the quick actions and decisions of my wife, Karrie, the support of my brother Matthew, my sons, Daniel, Mark and Stephen, our pastors, Claire Schlegel and Paul Knopf, and finally and importantly, the medical team. God has gifted humans with the ability to know and understand science and learn the art of medical treatment and the multiple disciplinary work of patient treatment and care. These efforts of the doctors, staff, family, and friends, such as David Collier, brought me through, and I have been determined every day since to discover that spark that I have fostered most of my life to live as a Christian. I want to look beyond the questions and confusions of religion and religious people and return to my foundational beliefs and practices.

Those beliefs do not include religion infused with politics or social positions and reactions. These interferences had turned me off some and made me feel somewhat alone in the church (not the local body we love so much), alone and worried that the church had become unhinged with its extremism and exclusivity.

Now, I don't worry about what others think of me and my own ideas or concerns about education, social justice, racism, or economic inequity. These are important things, but they are an individual perspective and a matter of each person's conscience. They aren't a litmus test to determine if a believer is genuine or not, as is apparently popular with some extremist individuals. These folks don't speak for me or the Christian church at large. They are merely a drop in the bucket of time and eternity and don't change what Jesus came as God's only son to do for humankind. Jesus died once for all people on the earth, and God has shown us his love in this way. When Jesus was raised from the dead, he demonstrated the victory of life over death that results from simple faith in his act of love and in a gracious God. No political populist message can steal that from me. Nor can the forces of intellect and education that I have in my background keep me from a childlike faith in Christ that has sustained me throughout my life.

For fifteen years I have experienced the disabling symptoms of a neurological syndrome that was labeled "so much more than Parkinson's disease" but required the same treatments. I had trouble thinking, walking, speaking, and eating. I shook almost constantly, and I was slowly, insidiously declining. While I was doing my best to maintain a positive outlook, I was struggling to determine what was left of my life in terms of time and the limited energy I had to act on my remaining dreams. This is my story—one of struggle, finding hope, and overcoming. Inch by inch, step by off-balance step, working my way back to a life that would bear a resemblance to the person I had been before my diagnosis.

I intended for this book to be a story about moving further along—not just forward, but with real hope. With it I have told how, through my precarious walk through disability and sickness, I found that, around every corner and in every circumstance, there was always another source of motivation to go on, a renewed sense of the drive to keep getting up each day, and a purpose for being the man I was and would continue to be.

As I recounted in earlier chapters, a year before deep brain stimulation surgery, I was provided information by my neurologist and instructed to begin to think about the possibility. I had time to watch DVD, read, and learn as much as I could. I talked to other patients. Eventually, I was ready to consider it, and at the same time, I was referred for a consultation with Dr. Merrill Morgan, the neurosurgeon who would eventually conduct the operation. As I wrote earlier, my steps brought me to the decision and the experience of going

through two surgical procedures that would complete
the process of deep brain stimulation in July of 2012.
These were pivotal events in bringing a positive change
into my life. Risky, yes—but sometimes what is needed
is real change to bring about the renewal that is desperately needed.

My desire is that as you have read about my process of growing and learned that you too can overcome
situations that seem impossible. Just maybe, from my
humble perspective, you will have gained a little insight
into how you may find hope in the most unexpected
experiences if you are willing to venture out like never
before. You might find, as I have in moving forward,
that there is always hope and the possibility of overcoming. I have always been a person who places a lot
of stock in finding purpose for one's life. In my own
case, I have strongly held beliefs in Christianity that
are central to my life. I have great respect for others
and their own sacred views and values. In this book, I
have spoken of faith in God, and with respect to each
reader, I do not propose to hold all knowledge, nor do
I consider myself better than others. I am simply a man
who places faith in a belief that has been planted and
watered and has grown to be the center of my being. I
received help from many over the years, but none could
be more important in that planting and watering phase
of my life than Rev. Dr. Jay Bartow, who was my associate minister at our home church growing up, Lakewood
First Presbyterian Church. Jay preached a sermon a few

years back, and to give you his perspective on how I know he helped make my life journey better than it ever could have been, I would like to share this excerpt from his message:

Last week Gail and I visited family and friends in Southern California, and one visit in particular warmed my heart. My first call was to a church in Long Beach where I was pastor to students. Early on I visited several high schools to meet students on their own turf. One afternoon after school I met a young man named Dan Brooks who was practicing free throws, and we struck up a conversation as we shot baskets. It turned out that he sporadically attended the church where I worked and I invited him to our high school group which was just about to begin a weekly Bible discussion group.

He was one of the first four to come, and the message of Christ connected with him and he began to invite others, and soon we had thirty-five students coming and seeing, to borrow the language of John's Gospel. And what they saw was the Spirit of Christ bringing hope and purpose and life to their fellow students.

Four and half years later I was called here to Monterey, but in the intervening years good things were happening in Dan's life and the lives of many others in that group. He worked as a youth pastor for a while and then as a public school teacher at the elementary level. He had a special charisma and touch with children and their parents. Later he worked his way into administration and personnel management in one of the top positions of a district. He and his wife raised three sons who are all doing well. But then Dan began to notice some physical problems which turned out to be the first stages of a Parkinson's-like illness which has cut short his work career.

But that doesn't stop Dan from serving and loving others. He has written a memoir and launched a blog titled wewillgoon.com. And that is what he does. On Thursdays he sings at a nearby convalescent hospital. That he gets there slowly and with a walker tells them it isn't easy, but he does it because he knows his visits bring some light to the residents there. He has made them part of his world.

At Dan's home I noticed a copy of Peterson's *The Message* that he had received this Christmas. When he reads that passage I cited earlier where Jesus says, "Walk with me and work with me—watch how I do it. Learn the unforced rhythms of grace. I won't lay anything heavy or ill-fitting on you. Keep company with me and you'll learn to live freely and lightly," I am certain he will say a loud "amen!"

Believe me; Pastor Jay did more for the other teens in our group and for me than we ever did for him! He was instrumental in helping me realize the important aspects of the faith journey that I could lay down as tracks for moving forward in my life. Not a year went by, as I married Karrie, we raised our sons, and I worked in my chosen profession, that I didn't reflect on things he had said and done to demonstrate the value of walking with God. And today Jay and I are walking together, further along, as he faces a serious lung disease called pulmonary fibrosis and is faced with losing his ability to do the sports and activities he has loved throughout his life. He rarely complains and always asks about others, showing interest in their joys, struggles, and sorrows. He encourages me to remember how much God loves me and seeks me to be the best I can, with the circumstances that I have to face. What an honor it is to have him as a dear friend and pal over a span of fifty years!

I hope that as you have read you have been encouraged to continue on your own journey to know and understand what you believe and hold dear. My intention is that what I have shared with you has added to your own sense of purpose and challenged you to seek the best for your life.

As a result of the desire I have always had to maintain my direction as a person who desires to walk with God, I have made faith in him the most powerful influencing factor in my goals and decisions. It was because of my Christian beliefs and desire to make a difference in the lives of others that I chose my career direction to be a teacher. My role as an upper elementary grades (fourth through sixth) teacher led to furthering my education in graduate school, which allowed me to pursue a leadership position as a school principal. I spent sixteen years as a site level administrator, with thirteen as a principal. At the apex of my career, I was leading leaders as a human resources administrator. In what would be my final role, I was recruiting, training, and negotiating with employees in a large-school system with nearly 8,000 students. I always wanted to know that what I was doing each day was having a positive impact on the lives of children and adults that I served. It was while I was in the middle of this role that I developed serious neurological symptoms.

I was caught completely off guard, with a world of plans yet to complete. I was looking forward to continuing my career when it was cut short by tremors throughout my body, slowed thinking, changes in my ability to walk, and trouble with coordinating my eye movements. This extrapyramidal syndrome and abnormal involuntary movement disorder brought a number of neurological symptoms that were gradually more and more disabling. Over time, I began to shake more and more, struggled to walk with balance and strength, and saw cognitive changes that made it harder for me to function. I was not able to continue to work, and driving was out of the question because of the danger I would present to others and myself. What does a guy do when he loses the career he loves and spent a life building, and the freedom to drive is no longer an option? I could easily have given up—slept until noon, taken my medication, and felt sorry for myself as I declined. It is important with a degenerative brain disease that you continue to use your mind and develop activities (or continue those you already had) that will help you to maintain your abilities as long as possible. A condition such as mine, identified as multiple systems atrophy and corticobasal syndrome, has a life expectancy of seven to fifteen years. This was a realization that took me from several months to a year to grasp and learn to face. When you discover that you have a fairly rare and serious condition, you must come to grips with the worst possible outcome, so for a year or so, I was quite aware that death was imminent and going through the grief that this brings.

I decided to go on with my life in the best possible way I knew how. I would educate others about my experience and what I was learning from it. In so doing, I was attempting to go on being the guy I had always been. My faith had prompted me to find purpose in things I could do for others. Teaching, singing, encouraging, and lifting hearts of people were things I could still accomplish. I set out to do those things!

I was very happily married, and my wife was an active part in encouraging me to do the things that I could do. Her support made all the difference and helped equip me with confidence and faith that I could still be a help to patients, caregivers, and people struggling with illness or other hardships. My sons Daniel, Mark, and Stephen, had always been my pride and joy and the sparkle in my eye. These three fine young men rose to the occasion and provided me with strength, companionship and confidence, enabling me to go on and overcome the challenges that we were all facing in our close-knit family. Our family is stronger and more resilient than ever as we walk through life together. We prioritize each other and stand shoulder to shoulder as each of us walks on in our lives as individuals—but as a committed family unit. When our first grand-child, Naomi, was born and then subsequently four more—Mariamne, William, Jack and Enid—we had special grandchildren to keep us busy and add to our happiness!

Our now-retired pastor, Rev. Dr. Brad Copeland, was always one to think of ways to encourage people to use their talents in service to others. He had lunch with me when I was deeply grieving about these chang-es. He asked what dream I had that I would like to accomplish while I could. I told him that I desired to record some more of my songs in a simple, acoustic format. Privately, he and some of our church's faith-ful friends gave us a wonderful financial contribution with the admonition to go and record! What started out as a simple idea lead to a project that grew into an album called "I Will Go On," named from the title song I wrote to express my decision to make the best of a hard situation. Karrie and our son, Mark, were both a part of this project, with Mark playing drums and singing background vocals and Karrie also singing on several of the songs. This was a great blessing and a wonderful gift by Pastor Brad and others in the church that were never identified. These friends just gave from their hearts and brought some joy into our lives that wouldn't have been there otherwise. Our friend Jeremy Shultz produced this album in his Lemon Lounge studio. I will forever be thankful that this project jump-started my life and helped me to move forward, rather than learning to be sick. This was a key "overcoming" moment.

Another choice I made was to begin to write. I thought I would investigate my disease and write about it for other patients. Also, I wanted to write about how I would go on in spite of a brain disease. I wanted to write a book but thought it would be a slow process. I wanted to get my message out instantly. The best avenue would be a blog site on the internet. I began to write articles on a website I called PD Plus Me. At the time, there were just a handful of people who had such a personal blog about Parkinson's-related syndromes and I had a unique area to write about since I had an atypical form of Parkinson's. I would research the various atypical parkinsonism syndromes and post my explanations I was creating with the benefit of books I was reading and internet research. This blog—which I eventually renamed We Will Go On—grew and grew, and soon 1,000 visits per month was the norm for my pages. In time, I would write that book I had hoped to, taking hundreds of pages from my blog and editing and rewriting them in a book form. I added an auto-biography as the last chapter in the back of this book and shared some of the stories that patients and care-givers had sent me in the middle. We edited the book ourselves—I reread the entire transcript two times and asked my wife to use her talent for detail to give it a thorough review—before submitting it for publishing. A lot of work but very rewarding. A three-year process of blogging, book writing, editing, and publishing was finally brought to fruition in March of 2009. This book opened some doors for me and brought people into our lives who we would never have met.

Meanwhile, we decided to do one more studio al-bum with some new songs I had been working on to be included—with some that I had worked on over the years. Our son, Mark, and my brother, Matthew, both played instruments on this album, which was eventu-ally named "Curtain Call." Mark's best friend—and a longtime friend of the family—Michael Bouska, was the engineer and editor of these special music tracks we laid down in his studio, located in the garage of his parents home. It was a two-year effort and resulted in a quality CD that included some of my best record-ed music of the songs that I have written. Mark pro-duced the album while Michael was the co-producer. Our son Stephen drew the cover portrait of me playing my guitar—a very nice personal touch. In the fall of 2009, Karrie helped me with a wonderful dessert and coffeehouse concert in our very own shady backyard in our last house, before we moved to our townhome where we reside presently. Several of our close friends and family came to enjoy an intimate acoustic performance of tunes from this newly released album. It was a great time, though emotional. One song, "Through Your Eyes," said it all as it began, "I'm sitting here wondering what to say, I'm sitting here wondering what to do, Knowing that my words, just won't be enough, to tell you, all you mean to me. I've watched the world as it changes. This isn't really a place I want to be. When the time arrives, it just won't be enough. To hold me the way you've held on to me."

This was a song with an honest message about the world seeming different in this state as a patient with a serious neurological disease and how I was going to go about facing life in this different form. Those were the steps I could take in that first few years of diagnosis and treatment for this atypical parkinsonism syndrome. Since the completion of "Curtain Call" and the publishing of my book *I Will Go On*, I have moved on to other areas of focus. And as you have read previously, I did go through with deep brain stimulation surgery and have had a renewed freedom as I have walked better and shaken less. It is not perfect, and there is no way to know how long some of these benefits will last, but I am grateful for every advantage it has brought. For several years, I returned to playing and singing music regularly at my church. In early 2020 I had surgery to place a tracheostomy tube in my throat and feeding tube into my abdomen. This past year, March 2020 through March 2021, I played in the virtual band for our church, recording and submitting videos of myself playing guitar and mandolin. I struggle to breathe and have given up solid food, save a bit of yogurt or thickened liquids.

I don't know what the future holds as I continue to face a neurodegenerative disease and the gradual decline that it brings, but I think I have learned to go on. I have put my head down, squared my shoulders, and trudged forward into the headwinds. I have grown to relish the adventure, learning to lean on others whose mutual love inspires me. And while continuing to lean on Jesus, my purpose and the rock of my being. Overcoming, not of my own doing, but of his.

CHAPTER TEN

Further Along

There comes a point in every person's life where you must face difficulties and pain. The question regards how you deal with that struggle: are you able to face it with faith and overcoming personal strength? I have found that, when I am dealing with illness or a large challenge, it is best for me to look for the opportunity within that situation.

This past year has been one of those times. I faced the potential of dying, and when I did, I emerged with a renewed sense of purpose and awareness of what I value most in life. Among those are family closeness, my marriage, and the desire for Christian interaction and the fellowship of friends. The latter I found in the form of an online men's Bible study group sponsored by First Presbyterian Church of Monterey and led by my close friend, Pastor Jay Bartow. This activity took me into in-depth study of scripture and the opportunity to develop new friendships and rediscover some old ones, namely Gary Edwards and Dana Seufert. I was glad to get to know and become good friends with Jay Jarman, Jim Trost, Jim Jenifer, and Jack Arnold. Though a virtual group, there is nothing virtual about these relationships. This study group has been priceless, and these are friends I consider very dear.

Our family was heavily impacted by the loss of ability to spend time together due to COVID-19 and the social distance requirements that resulted. Thus, this year has been one of isolation and longing for more closeness with our sons, daughters-in-law, and grandchildren.

When I look back on all that has happened since I became ill with a degenerative brain disease, it seems remarkable that I have been able to live so well, for so long. Even now, with brain implants, a battery in my upper right chest, a G-tube for feeding me a liquid diet, and a tracheostomy, I am living a life that is full of joy and many possibilities for each day.

I have to say that Karrie makes all the difference. She is my romantic partner but also truly my best friend and my caregiver. Really she is a nurse without the title. I am not taking anything away from those who have the degree, training, and experience to become registered nurses or licensed vocational nurses. It is just that nurses visit our home and have said that Karrie is functioning quite well in her nursing capacity.

Others have said that few spouses could do the kinds of things for their loved one that she does for me.

Changing out a trach tube once each month is an awesome responsibility and a bit unnerving. There is a bit of pain involved, and Karrie has worked it out so that the pain is minimal to very little as it goes in the stoma leading to my trachea. She and I have a system for this and a number of things. The cleaning of the area around my trach each morning and the changing of the inner cannula are small by comparison, but they are daily and persistent chores that she takes on gladly. Cleaning around my G-tube each morning is equally time consuming and tedious. She must make judgements with each area to determine if she is seeing anything discharged that is possibly infected or unusual in my case. She then takes care of decisions that would need to be made and determines whether I should be seen by a doctor.

There are a number of other daily issues and occasional ones. The regular feedings, as I have said, take place three times each day. There is a tedious process of connecting several tubes and valves to infuse the thick liquid food into my stomach directly—it provides my complete nourishment. She is dedicated to routine, and that takes a lot of discipline, which she has in droves. My oxygen concentrator is worn nonstop with a few occasional interruptions. This is done either through a nasal cannula or a trach mask over my tracheostomy.

The few times per week that I don't have it connected to my throat or nasal passages, she maintains awareness of my blood oxygen level with the oximeter device she places on my finger. With multiple system atrophy the heart rate can slow quite a bit, and has reached into the mid to high forties this last year, and it is at fifty-five or so beats per minute several times each day when least expected. Before I had this disease, my heart rate was in the high seventies to low eighties and remained there as my brain provided the controlling impulses to see to that status. Without the autonomic system working properly, the heart rate must be monitored along with my oxygen, so Karrie stays on top of that too.

There are more tasks and responsibilities like this than I can list here, but there are some additional special concerns and tasks that being my willing caregiver requires. The medical supplies need to be managed, and this adds hours to the week and many compounded hours to each month. Karrie has a cart dedicated to my trach, breathing, and feeding needs. She orders and maintains a supply chain for each of the various components of my trach care, which include but are not limited to 1) replacement trach kits, inner cannula replacements; 2) neck tie for the trach flange; 3) gauze, saline water; 4) various tubing for feeding and oxygen; 5) the boxes and boxes of liquid diet; 6) the rental and maintenance of equipment, such as the hospital bed I sleep in; 7) the oxygen concentrator machine; 8) portable oxygen and tanks; 9) the transfer wheelchair for going out in the car; 9) the nebulizer for treating my wind pipe and lungs twice daily; 10) the suction machine; and 11) suction catheters to suction mucus and unwanted fluid and particles from my trachea and tracheostomy. Much of this is kept on a very well-organized cart that rolls. I can only imagine what a nightmare a home could be without a clean, disciplined, and organized person to handle all these and many other issues.

The hardest challenge is her needing to be vigilant about the possibility of my having an emergency breathing crisis. I have these occasionally, and since being home from the nursing home in the winter of 2020, one such crisis I described previously was serious enough that Karrie determined the need to send me by ambulance to the emergency room, where I stayed overnight and was given care for twenty-four hours. This resulted in the now steady diet of oxygen that we maintain on a permanent basis. Karrie keeps an eye open, figuratively, as she sleeps, in the event that something happened at night, such as a constriction of my air way, a cognitive lapse, or a serious anxiety attack that accompanies my brain illness and misperceptions that one could refer to as paranoia. Sometimes she gets up to give me Tylenol just to quell the pain in my neck stoma that is keeping me awake. She watches carefully if I get out of bed at night to be sure I don't fall or forget to put my oxygen back on after I return to climb in the sheets.

The emotional toll of all of these things—not only the work, but because of the fact that she truly loves me and I her—is overwhelming. Karrie has to deal with her own medical needs too, which thankfully aren't life threatening but are important none the less. As a result, depression, anxiety, loneliness, anger, grief, and loss of freedom are all a big part of who she is in these times. I am so thankful for her counting my various medications each and every day, ordering them, maintaining the stock, and keeping it all refilled on a continuing basis. I can say I would do the same for her if the roles were reversed, because I love her just as much as she does me. I can also say that I would not be as good at these tasks and responsibilities because she is so gifted in organization and self-discipline that she makes this all go so smoothly. What a wonder she is, and I thank her daily as many times as humanly possible. She is truly God's goodness to me in my life.

We are enjoying our grown children and their spouses and are so proud of all of them and their progress in life. Each of our sons is employed and excellent at their professions and roles within them. Each of their spouses is a great partner and highly intelligent as well. They are close to us, and we treat these wonderful women as our "own" children. We thank their kind parents for sharing their special daughters! We have five, going on six, grandchildren about whom we are over the moon. They are the best part of our early senior years! There are three, going on four girls and two boys. If I do say so myself, these kids are all brilliant, have special abilities, and are fun to be around. We treasure the times we spend with everyone, and we will soon have fourteen when we sit at the table on family days when the COVID-19 pandemic is finally fully controlled and somewhat "over." It will never be truly over, in my humble opinion.

I worry about the family and their feelings about what is going on in my body and brain. I know it is taxing, and my sons, Daniel, Mark, and Stephen, have had to face serious illness and medical crises with me much earlier than I did with my parents. I don't know what it is like to be in their shoes—worrying while their father is in ICU on a trach and ventilator. As I said earlier, they were there for me, but even more, they were there for their mother—giving her a shoulder to lean on, an ear to listen, and a word of encouragement or input on a decision. We are so fortunate to have our sons, their wives, and their children. How blessed we are!

This past year was exceptionally difficult as my father was declining in health and we weren't sure why, other than aging, until the few months prior to his passing. For years, apparently, my dad had prostate cancer. When he checked into the veteran's hospital, it was discovered that he had metastatic prostate cancer that had moved into his spine, hips—and who knows where else in his body? My brother, Matthew, and sister, Teri, were willing to generously move in with him for several months at a time and worked in tandem to care for Dad in the last several months together. Our sister was visiting for a month or two twice each year the last several years, providing company and support before we knew why Father was in the pain he was describing. Our brother Casey made two trips out from South Carolina to spend time with Dad this last year of his life. I know Dad appreciated that effort and those hours spent together. So, in October 2020, my dear father, Ronald Brooks, passed on. I have great faith that his belief in Jesus Christ will be rewarded with an eternity in heaven and have hope that I will be reunited with him and my mother, Marguerite Brooks, someday, as well.

Going through the near-death experience, along with the challenges of living with a deep brain system in place—dependence on a tracheostomy and feeding tube, plus a degenerative brain condition limiting my mobility and bodily functions—has made 2020–2021 and the years that follow a greater and greater challenge. I find my solace in the realization that I have lived a good life and have been blessed with a wonderful immediate family, loving extended family, a number of great friends, the most supportive church community you could find anywhere, a career in public education that meant the world to me, a life in music as a performer, singer, musician and songwriter, and provisions for living that include everything we need to sustain us and shelter us. I am a fortunate man, and I intend to keep moving forward, further along—ultimately I know where this journey leads.

CHAPTER 11

Gratitude

Throughout this past year, after coming home from the Compassionate Care skilled nursing facility, I have had a great deal of up times, along with some down times. The good far outweigh the bad. I would like to mention some of the opportunities and people who have been there for me through this year and a half.

I was home a week or two, when the music leader, Saw Shein, contacted me and said to feel free to record my guitar and mandolin anytime. They had begun virtual worship and praise, and the contemporary service team was being included for three songs each week. I jumped right on that train, trach and all, recording videos in my little home studio on my computer. Early on, I did some solo songs and played a few featured tunes, with Saw himself supporting me with his great piano and vocals. Pastor Paul Knopf helped me with submitting the video recordings to Dropbox and was there to support my efforts to complete the project for each week. These guys were there encouraging me every step of the way. Though I could not leave home much due to my tracheostomy and feeding tube, along with my inability to walk much at all or drive, I could still play my instruments—guitar and mandolin—and be dependable for a year as I answered that call. Thank you, Saw and Paul, for honoring me with that opportunity.

My associate minister from my hometown church in Lakewood, California, Reverend Dr. Jay Bartow, established contact with me three years before my breathing crisis. He and his wife, Gail Bartow, came down twice to visit Karrie and me. We enjoyed visiting and having them in our home. They were so generous with their time, and they went out of their way to make these visits possible. Though Jay and I had occasionally exchanged letters all through the forty-five years since he had left Southern California, we had only seen each other once in 1977 when I visited his home briefly. Now, we were in touch and in contact for almost three years leading up to my crisis. We were talking weekly and enjoying our friendship. When I came home from Compassionate Care, Jay, as the retired pastor emeritus of First Presbyterian Church of Monterey, invited me to attend a virtual, online Bible study fellowship. This met weekly on Tuesdays. As stated previously, I agreed to participate and have been involved in that for a year and am still going. Through Jay, I have met twenty to thirty men who are very sincere, solid people with a devotion to their faith and meaningful lives with great experiences and insight to share. It has been a great pleasure to be a part of that, and it has strengthened my faith to do so, as I wrote earlier in the book. I appreciate all of the men in the group, though it has been nice to also spend time with two old friends, Dana Seufert and Gary Edwards, who also participated in Reverend Jay Bartow's youth group in Lakewood. I have missed them, and it was so wonderful to be a part of one another's lives in this way, particularly during this year of a pandemic called COVID-19.

Jay and I are great friends and closer than ever, having established our relationship back when I was in high school. I conveyed earlier how he jogged by me at school, practicing free throws one evening. Today, Jay and I speak regularly outside of the Bible study group, and we consider each other pals. What a blessing he is to Karrie and me.

I want to state again that we have had visiting nurses that have supported us. We have been very appreciative of Rebecca, our nurse practitioner from the palliative care organization, who watches over my health monthly or more. Tina has also been a home health nurse and supported us most every week through the year. We appreciate the kindness and expertise these professionals have shown.

There have been hard times. Pain and difficulty breathing, more during some times than others. I reviewed earlier how, one night in October, I couldn't get a breath and Karrie called the paramedics. My heart rate dropped down dramatically, and the EMTs were artificially forcing oxygen into my lungs to keep me going until they could drive me by ambulance to the hospital, where I spend a night and a total of twenty-four hours. This occurrence, ten months after coming home, meant that, from that point on, I would be hooked up to oxygen most of the time. I receive it through a tube coming from an oxygen concentrator. I either wear a trach mask over my trach—or in recent weeks, I have used a nasal cannula to receive the oxygen. This has further restricted my movement and freedom to go out. Meanwhile, the COVID-19 outbreak has caused the whole country, along with the world, to take social distancing and PPE precautions, so it is hard to interact much at all. I came home just in time to avoid being locked down in the nursing home, separated from my lovely wife and dear sons and their families, but it has been a lonely year for Karrie and me. We have great times talking and doing things that we enjoy. I keep playing and learning on my instruments and electronic recording devices. I have been making my own videos of various songs to share with those who might enjoy hearing my offerings, though at this stage they are humble and limited by parkinsonian movement problems and difficulty with hand control, which forces me to fight while playing instruments.

We have been happy that, with careful social distancing, we have visited as well as possible in small groups with our three sons, Mark, Daniel, and Stephen and their families. Mark and Sarah bring William and Enid over regularly while masked, and we responsibly are visiting a bit more each month as the vaccines are being administered and the picture is very slowly improving. Daniel, with his daughters, Naomi and Mariamne, has come over every Sunday after church to visit and spend time together. These visits are made even more special the many times that Jenny, Daniel's wife, has been able to join us. Karrie prepares crafts and activities, and I get to see our granddaughters while having a nice talk with Daniel. Stephen and Kelley, with their son, Jack, live farther away and have come down as much as possible. Recent months have limited our time together, but we have a very regular weekly FaceTime video call with the three of them and have had the chance to watch Jack grow and progress in his interests and abilities. Our grandchildren are our pride and joy!

I mentioned previously how my sister, Teri, and brother, Matthew, were so instrumental in taking major time from their lives to go and live with our father for most of 2020. They took care of him and assisted the caregivers that I arranged through the veteran's care coordinator program he qualified for as a result of his participation in the Korean War. I will never be able to thank Matt and Teri enough for all that they gave and the way that they did all they could to ease our father's pain in this last year of our father's life. Thank you both so much, and I love you.

Today I am keeping busy, writing, practicing music, and trying whenever I can to make videos. I already explained how it has become necessary in recent months for me to have a more restrictive kind of trach tube installed. I have had a smooth trach tube, but in order for it to be placed on a ventilator at night while sleeping or in the daytime, while napping, I need a cuffed trach. This is a tube with a ridge around the bottom, which is down in the stoma but also contains an attached ring which is inflatable. This inflatable ring is filled with air through a plastic syringe by Karrie when being placed on the ventilator, which will mean I cannot speak while the ring is inflated. After the daily time spent using the inflated, cuffed trach, Karrie will deflate it in order to give me some freedom to speak. I don't yet know if the deflated ring will restrict air flow to my vocal cords, but I am hopeful that I will be able to keep speaking well enough to be understood adequately. As I write this, I have now had this cuffed tracheostomy replacement procedure and am adjusting to it being in my airway. It was not as smooth a transition as I would have hoped, with pain and discharge around the area, but it now has improved after nearly six weeks. Soon the ventilator will be delivered, and we will begin using it. By the time we print this book, it will be known how this went.

I am anxious but full of hope and exercising faith. I am a faulty human being, and I certainly do not have all the answers. My humanness means that

I am sometimes disillusioned and confused. I hold onto my faith in these times, even if by my fingernails while hanging from the edge of a roof. I know God loves us and has plans to bring fulfillment through our relationships with those we care most about and his love and grace for and toward us. I will close with this: 2020–2021 has been a difficult time, but there have been rewards.

Many good people, all of whom I cannot list here, have given of themselves in ways I never could if the tables were reversed. Not because I wouldn't want to, but because of my physical and cognitive limitations. My new friend, Jay Jarman, from the morning Bible study online group, explained it this way in the notes I took that morning: "Dan, gratitude is your superpower. You are characterized by gratitude above all other characteristics. Someday I can see you standing before your savior, Jesus, and telling him how much gratitude you have for his love and grace toward you. Just hold on to that thought."

I will indeed.

Acronyms, Terms, and Abbreviations

AH - Alzheimer's disease

ALS - amyotrophic lateral sclerosis (Lou Gehrig's Disease)

CBD - corticobasal degeneration

CBGD - corticobasal ganglionic degeneration

CBS - corticobasal syndrome

DaT - dopamine transporter scan

DBS - deep brain stimulation

FTD - frontotemporal degeneration

G Tube - gastrostomy tube

LBD - Lewy body dementia

MRSA - Methicillin-resistant Staphylococcus aureus

MRI - magnetic resonance imaging

MSA - multiple system atrophy

MSA-C - multiple system atrophy, cerebellar

MSA-P - multiple system atrophy, parkinsonism

PBA - psuedobulbar affective disorder

PD - Parkinson's disease

PEG Tube - percutaneous endoscopic gastrostomy
PET - positron emission tomography
PSP - progressive supranuclear palsy
SND - striatonigral degeneration
Trach - tracheostomy

A Portrait

Can't see him or hear him just now
But his image is strong in my mind
I know how he sounds, how he looks and he feels
With this image of Dan on my mind.

Let me tell you about him as I know him best
And this image for you might be real.

So serious about life and the future spread before him
Quality…reality…pure motives
But not searching for truth, for He is in his heart
While he seeks to perform well in all He requires.
Running the race for the high calling of God
Running for life and spirit
On and on…
At times he tires, but there's more.

That wooden floor
The courtship of a court
A romance that would come and go
Only to return in dreams and special times.
For Dan, the high-top award of enthusiasm.
Himself a singer of songs
Lender of the Lyric
Writer of Words
This a dream?
No, it's real to hear him…to see him…to enjoy!

The psalmist and Saul
Lewis and the shadow
Tempt him away from his work
Escaping for a moment
To the lands of their worlds
Of old, and of new, and of now.
The bearer of sons
Not from the womb but from the soul
To them, all he knows he'll pass on.
Requiring his time, patience and love
He reads a bit less but loves a bit more.

Then I step in
The winner's running mate
Not always in stride but not far behind
To watch and admire in a starry-eyed state.
He loves me and helps in all I might try

This teacher of the young
My mentor as well.
The commitment of a lifetime
A promise of faith
Together, we enter and press on
Together, we'll see life through
Together, this portrait completes.

CPSIA information can be obtained
at www.ICGtesting.com
Printed in the USA
LVHW011137230721
693494LV00019B/1034/J